Columbia River

COLUMBIA RIVER
Gateway to the West

Text and Principal Color Photography by CARLOS ARNALDO SCHWANTES

Additional Color Photography by Steve Eltinge and Ralph Lee Hopkins

COLUMBIA RIVER MARITIME MUSEUM
Astoria, Oregon

UNIVERSITY OF IDAHO PRESS
Moscow, Idaho

FRONTIS: *Cruising at sunrise in mid-May 1997 between Astoria and the mouth of the Columbia River.*

Columbia River: Gateway to the West
Copyright © 2000 by the University of Idaho Press
Copublished by the University of Idaho Press and the Columbia River Maritime Museum

Research was funded in part by the John Calhoun Smith Memorial Committee of the University of Idaho.

All rights reserved.
Design by Trina Stahl
Printed in Hong Kong.

All photographs are by the author, except where otherwise noted.

Library of Congress Cataloging-in-Publication Data
Schwantes, Carlos A., 1945–
Columbia River : gateway to the West / text and principal color photography by Carlos Arnaldo Schwantes ; additional color photography by Steve Eltinge and Ralph Lee Hopkins.
p.   cm.
Includes bibliographical references (p.   ).
ISBN 0-89301-218-1 (alk. paper)
1. Columbia River—History.   2. Columbia River—Description and travel.   3. Columbia River Pictorial works.   I. Title.
F853.S39   2000
979.7—dc21   99-33290
                                                                              CIP

Dedicated to my brothers, Dave and Jon, two of the most important people in my life.

CONTENTS

OPPOSITE: *Commercial navigation up the Columbia River from the Pacific Ocean ends here at the bridges linking Pasco and Kennewick, Washington.*

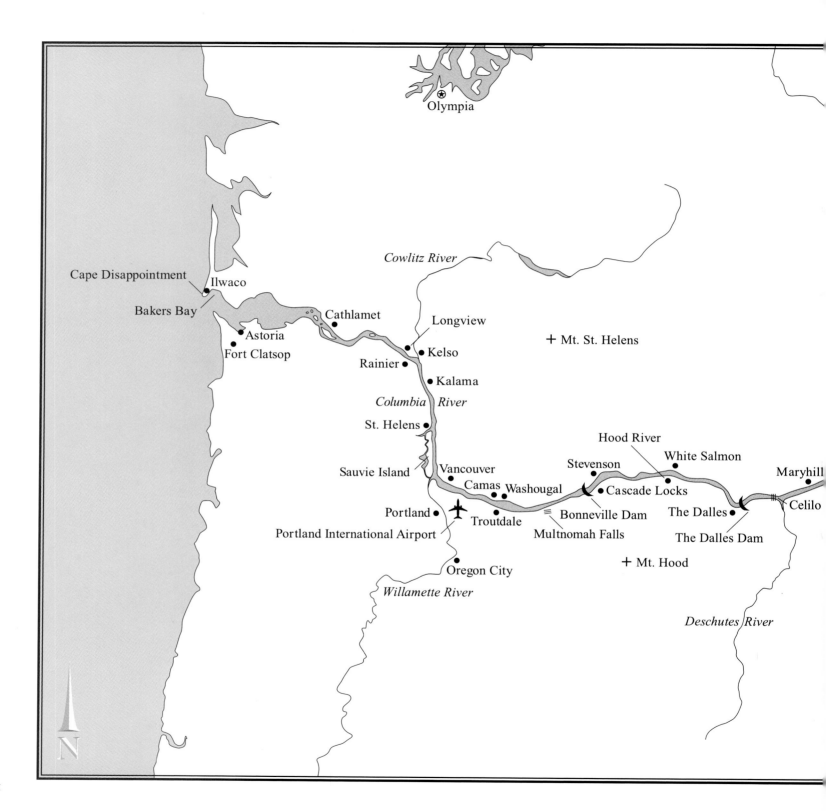

Olympia

Cape Disappointment
Ilwaco

Bakers Bay

Cowlitz River

Cathlamet

Longview

Astoria
Fort Clatsop

Kelso

Rainier

Kalama

Columbia   River

St. Helens

Hood River

White Salmon

Stevenson

Maryhill

Sauvie Island

Vancouver

Mt. St. Helens

Camas   Washougal

Cascade Locks

Portland

Troutdale

Bonneville Dam

The Dalles

Celilo

Portland International Airport

Multnomah Falls

The Dalles Dam

Oregon City

Mt. Hood

Willamette River

Deschutes River

N

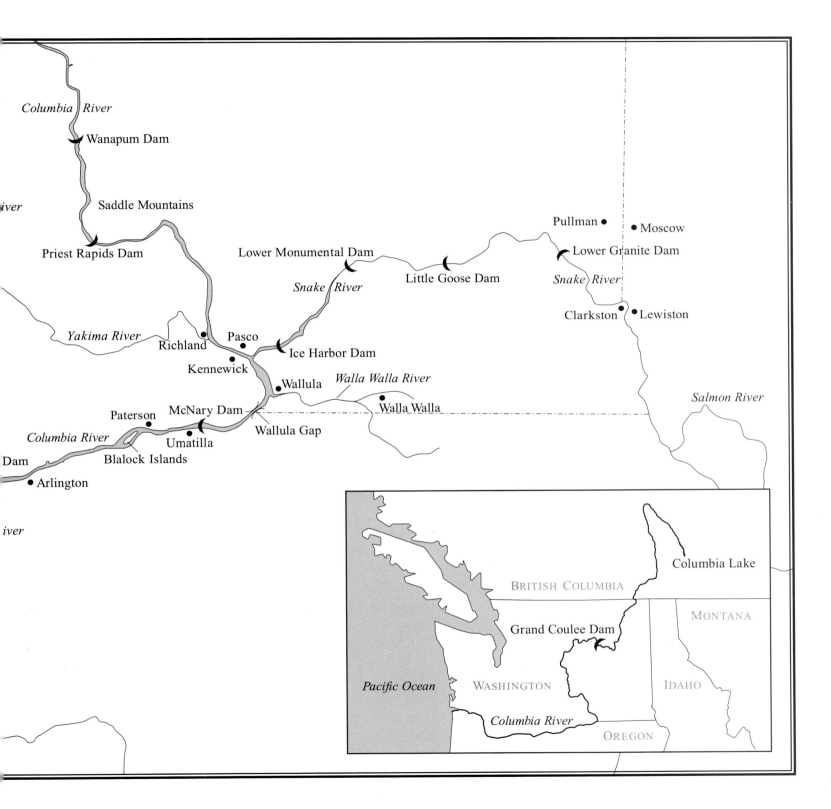

Columbia River

Wanapum Dam

Saddle Mountains

iver

Priest Rapids Dam

Pullman •   • Moscow

Lower Monumental Dam   Lower Granite Dam

Little Goose Dam   Snake River

Snake River

Yakima River   Clarkston •Lewiston

Richland •   • Pasco

Kennewick   Ice Harbor Dam

Wallula   Walla Walla River   Salmon River

McNary Dam   • Walla Walla

Paterson   Wallula Gap

Columbia River

Umatilla

Dam   Blalock Islands

• Arlington

iver

Columbia Lake

BRITISH COLUMBIA

MONTANA

Grand Coulee Dam

Pacific Ocean   WASHINGTON

IDAHO

Columbia River

OREGON

List of Illustrations

FOREWORD

FOR YEARS, visitors to the Columbia River Maritime Museum in Astoria have been requesting a book about the Columbia River and its maritime history. As a way to take home the magnificent images of the Columbia that visitors to the region witness in their travels, or furnish more details of the superb collections and exhibits in the Museum, or nourish a particular passion for the steamboat era, sailing ships, or fishing heritage of the Columbia River, such a book would also provide welcome details about the history of the "Great River of the West."

I have often looked for such a book myself, to share with friends and family members who do not live at the mouth of the Columbia. Living and working here, I have been fortunate to experience the river from the decks of a cruise ship, traveling upriver to Lewiston, Idaho, and down through Hells Canyon on a jet boat. I have enjoyed many quiet weekends exploring the backwaters of the lower river on my small sailboat, and I have crossed the notorious Columbia River Bar in both large ships and small craft. I've experienced violent seas with the U.S. Coast Guard on training and search-and-rescue missions and donned scuba gear to explore shipwrecks in the mouth of the river. Flying over the river, I have marveled at the complexity of its geography.

OPPOSITE: *Upper Horsetail Falls in the Columbia Gorge.*

Portrait of Rolf Klep, founder, benefactor, and early director of the Columbia River Maritime Museum. Columbia River Maritime Museum copy photo by Steve Eltinge (1982.28).

Yet I have never found just the right book to express the essence of the Columbia River, its personality and living characteristics as a river at once beautiful, changeable, and wildly dangerous. At some point, I realized that the book we all wanted would be a natural project for the Columbia River Maritime Museum. And then, as good fortune would have it, the person ideally suited to write this book walked into my office one day.

Carlos Schwantes enjoys a reputation far beyond his professional duties at the University of Idaho's Department of History. He is a far-ranging writer of Northwest history, an interpretive historian, and a passionate landscape photographer. His particular interest in transportation history was stimulated by several summers spent as ship historian aboard Columbia River cruise ships. Emphasizing the importance of the Columbia's commercial history, Carlos also shared his passionate excitement for the historical landscape. He has taken, by his own admission, thousands of photographs gleaned through years of patient work along the Columbia's banks and channels. Photographs contributed by outstanding professional photographers Steve Eltinge and Ralph Lee Hopkins complement Carlos' text and images.

At the Columbia River Maritime Museum, our primary purpose is to enrich lives by inspiring interest in the maritime history and culture of the Columbia River. We invite you aboard to enjoy the story and images of this Great River of the West as you come along on a voyage of discovery.

JERRY L. OSTERMILLER
Executive Director
Columbia River Maritime Museum, Astoria

Personal Perspectives

For more than a quarter of a century the Columbia River has loomed large in my life. Before I relocated from Ann Arbor, Michigan, to the Walla Walla, Washington, area in 1969, it essentially defined my mental images of the Pacific Northwest as a result of a youthful fondness for *National Geographic* magazines. When I finally did encounter the Great River of the West, its immensity left me both awed and speechless. During the past decade I have enjoyed two dozen journeys along more than four hundred miles of waterway between Astoria and Lewiston to give history lectures aboard cruise ships, and each time I found the Columbia River just as engaging as that first encounter. It was on such a trip in 1995 that I visited Jerry Ostermiller's office at the Columbia River Maritime Museum to pay my respects to a fellow Idahoan. He surprised me with a request to write the text for this book. Along with photographers Steve Eltinge and Ralph Lee Hopkins, I tried to capture with my camera the many moods of the river.

Of the dozen or so books I have previously written on the Pacific Northwest, none afforded me the luxury of concentrating exclusively on the Columbia River. The process of writing and researching the present book was thus much like an extended visit with an old friend. It revealed

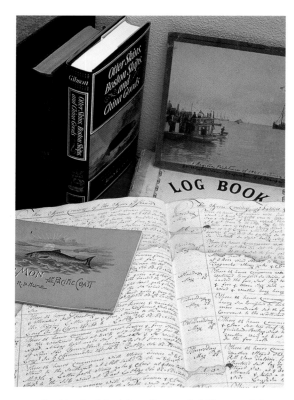

Inside the Maritime Research Library of the
Columbia River Maritime Museum. Columbia
River Maritime Museum photo by Steve Eltinge.

material new to me and provided an opportunity to revisit notes made initially for earlier books. In the end it was a challenging assignment to say so little about so big a topic. I only hope my "responsible reductionism" captured the essence of the Columbia River's historical landscape, especially the portion from The Dalles to Astoria. In any case, I take full responsibility for any errors of omission or fact.

I want to thank Jerry for offering me this assignment and also his always friendly and capable staff members for assisting me in so many different ways. I appreciate too the help and encouragement provided by Peggy Pace and her colleagues at the University of Idaho Press. Finally, the Columbia River Maritime Museum offered me its guest quarters aboard the lightship *Columbia.* The introductory paragraphs in chapter one were made on a bright but chilly morning in January 1996, when after a pleasant night aboard the lightship I arose early to survey the river at dawn. It was an unforgettable experience.

CARLOS A. SCHWANTES
University of Idaho

PORTFOLIO OF FAVORITE IMAGES

Fall colors burnish the Columbia Gorge in November 1998.

Morning sun causes lush vegetation in the Columbia Gorge to glisten.

At Cape Horn near the western entrance to the Columbia Gorge. The storm clouds of a November day lifted just before sunset.

Part of the power generation complex at Bonneville Dam.

Above Hood River on a windy September day.

A rustic mailbox near Mosier, Oregon.

~ *A sculpted landscape near Maryhill, Washington.*

At Umatilla the Columbia River widens until it merges with the sky.

Locking through McNary Dam in October 1998.

Contrast between land and sky near McNary Dam.

Dramatic Wallula Gap just before a storm in May 1999.

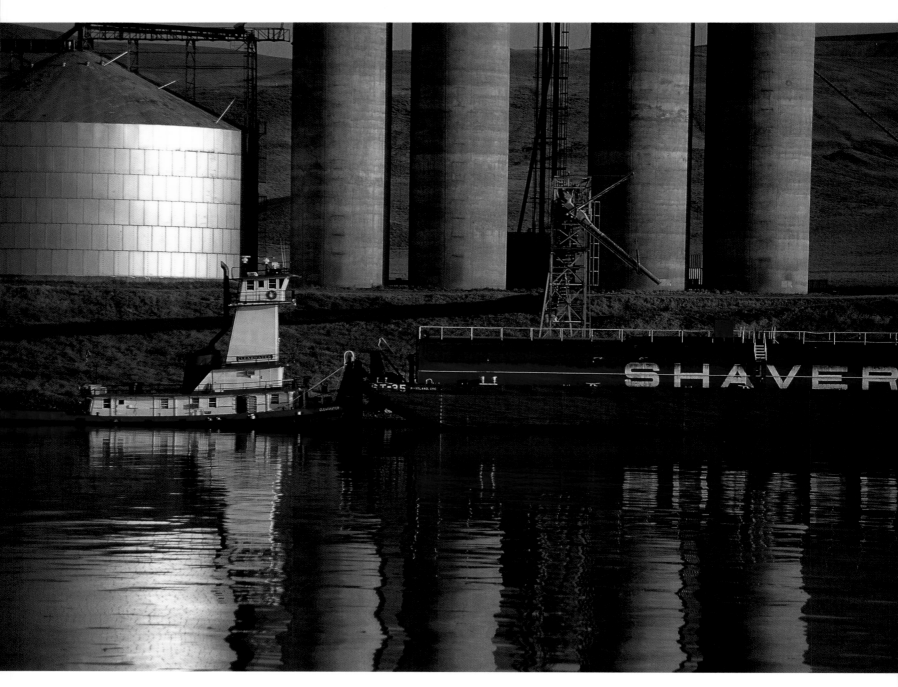

Loading grain on the Snake River near Central Ferry, Washington.

Basaltic headlands along the Snake River below Lewiston, Idaho, in November 1996.

Industrial art? Part of the Columbia River waterfront in Vancouver, Washington.

The industrial landscape of Portland along the Willamette River.

Self-portrait in Portland, November 1991.

COLUMBIA RIVER

GATEWAY TO THE WEST

THE FIRST LIGHT of a new day burnishes the broad expanse of water and causes it to sparkle like polished brass as it flows past the Columbia River Maritime Museum, and then almost disappears at the end of its journey from the Rocky Mountains to the Pacific Ocean. To my left are the lingering lights of Astoria and the nearly five-mile-long bridge that arches toward the sky and then nearly disappears from view before it reaches the distant Washington shore. Beyond the horizon and about twenty miles away lie Cape Disappointment and the far fringe of North America, where the Columbia River has its often tempestuous rendezvous with the open sea. Directly opposite me, a mile or two from shore and brightly lit like miniature cities, are several large ships at anchor. Off to my right and more than twelve hundred miles beyond the shadowy bulk of Tongue Point is where the Great River of the West originates as melting snow high in the Rocky Mountains of British Columbia. This modest stream gathers the waters of dozens of other rivers and streams so that by the time it flows past

OPPOSITE: *Sunrise at Tongue Point, a landmark located just upriver from Astoria.*

RIGHT: *Cape Disappointment lighthouse on the Washington side of the river.*

Astoria's waterfront it has drained a portion of the globe larger than France, Belgium, and the Netherlands combined—a drainage area of more than 250,000 square miles.

When describing the "Empire of the Columbia," it is easy to pile one impressive statistic on another until the mass of data benumbs the mind. I prefer to contemplate the river on a far more personal level, musing that when I take a shower at home in Moscow, Idaho, some of the water drains down Paradise Creek and into the Palouse River, which joins the Snake River and finally the Columbia. Here it mixes with water used by residents from communities as distant from one another as Eugene, Oregon, is from Revelstoke, British Columbia, or Kelso, Washington, is from Jackson, Wyoming. We bathers may live in two countries, seven different states, and several thousand distinct communities—and most of us will never meet face to face—but we have the Columbia in common.

Its waters knit together various parts of the Pacific Northwest more than any other physical feature, coursing through deserts, high plains, wheat fields, cattle ranges, grasslands, and forests as they twist their way between mountains to reach the sea. Over the years the Columbia River has

~ LEFT: *Today Palouse Falls is a Washington state park, one of the many natural wonders of the Columbia River and the vast landscape it encompasses.*

~ ABOVE: *An image of Palouse Falls published in 1863 in Captain John Mullan's* Report on the Construction of a Military road from Fort Walla-Walla to Fort Benton. *This eastern Washington landmark was popular with artists. A short distance below here its waters join the Snake River. Courtesy University of Idaho Library, Day-Northwest Collection (UA 963 A5 1863).*

Entrance to the Columbia River Maritime Museum in Astoria, Oregon. The massive anchor is from an Illinois-class battleship.

served as a vital transportation link and highway of history; a source of food, irrigation water, and hydroelectric power; a cause for environmental concern; and a dramatic regional symbol.

When it finally reaches Astoria, the Great River of the West is some four miles wide and a hundred feet deep in places. From my vantage point on the deck of the lightship *Columbia* it forms the centerpiece of a landscape rich in natural beauty. But there is also much that I cannot see: just a few feet beneath its glistening surface is a dark, primordial world that only a few specialists know. This is the concealed realm of the giant white sturgeon (North America's largest freshwater fish), wrecks like the brig *Isabella,* and who knows what else.

In much the same way, the Columbia River's rich historical landscape remains largely invisible to casual or first-time observers. On its south bank in Astoria stands the Columbia River Maritime Museum, whose primary goal is to make the invisible landscape of the river both vivid and accessible. The roofline of the building suggests cresting waves, while its outside walls are sheathed with weathered cedar shakes that reinforce the feel of the old canneries that once lined the Astoria waterfront. Even the street address of the Columbia River Maritime Museum recalls a date worth remembering: 1792 Marine Drive. It was on May 11, 1792, that an American merchant sea captain, Robert Gray of the *Columbia Rediviva,* sailed a short distance up the majestic waterway he named for his ship. Inside the museum building are twenty-five thousand square feet of exhibits that illuminate all important facets of the river's rich and varied history.

The geographic location of the Columbia River Maritime Museum is equally significant: Astoria and the lower Columbia River form the historic gateway to Oregon and the Pacific Northwest. This is a landscape filled with first encounters and early-day events of lasting importance in American history. Consider, for example, why the international boundary does not extend down the middle of the Columbia River instead of being anchored farther north along the forty-ninth parallel. A British or Canadian flag might well be flying on the opposite shore had it not been for

THE COLUMBIA RIVER MARITIME MUSEUM

Gateway to History

THE COLUMBIA RIVER MARITIME MUSEUM offers one of the most extensive collections of nautical artifacts on the West Coast. Its seven galleries and Great Hall are filled with paintings, ship models, and hundreds of artifacts that include fishing boats, Coast Guard rescue craft, Indian canoes, and marine engines. There is also the navigation bridge from the destroyer USS *Knapp* and the periscopes and a torpedo from the USS *Rasher*. Thousands of historical photographs and documents complete the picture of this area's maritime past. The names of the current galleries suggest the scope of the Museum's vision: Fur Trade and Exploration; Navigation and Marine Safety; Fishing, Canning, and Whaling; On the River; Sailing Vessels; Steam and Motor Vessels; and Naval History. Its educational programs seek to enhance visits by schoolchildren and the general public even as the museum extends its reach well beyond the Astoria area with "The Quarterdeck," a quarterly newsletter published since 1973. A maritime research library contains numerous ships' logs and documents and a comprehensive reference collection.

This remarkable treasury of maritime history is in large measure a tribute to the vision of Rolf Klep. This Portland native's name may not be a household word, but his technical illustrations have attracted and delighted millions of Americans, including the readers of *Colliers, Life, Look, Time*, and *National Geographic*. His painting of the luxury liner SS *United States*, originally commissioned by *Life* magazine and now on display in the Steam and Motor Vessels gallery, reveals a wealth of architectural detail by means of cutaway views of the ship's interior.

Klep's interest in Astoria's maritime heritage was his first inspiration. While on a trip around the world, he visited several major maritime museums in Europe which further heightened his interest in establishing their counterpart on the lower Columbia River. His vision took shape on May 11, 1962, when the Columbia River Maritime Museum was formally organized. Twenty years later to the day—and less than a year after Klep had passed away—the current museum building on the Astoria waterfront was dedicated. The Columbia River Maritime Museum has been fully accredited with the American Association of Museums since 1972.

a fateful encounter between the American Navy and the narrow channels, sandbars, and tricky currents at the river's mouth in 1841.

The Columbia bar. Those few words once struck inordinately great fear in the hearts of mariners. Treacherous sandbars and swirling currents caused much dread a hundred years ago. Even at the end of the twentieth century, with modern aids to navigation, dredging, and Coast Guard protection, the "Graveyard of the Pacific" commands respect from pilots and masters of vessels both large and small who must carefully calculate winds, tides, and currents to predict the best time to cross the Columbia bar safely. Thousands of boats and ships have been lost on the bar over the years. In recent times, the Coast Guard has saved countless numbers of vessels and lives. It launches two to three hundred rescue missions each year, though the bar still claims an average of six lives annually.

"Mere description," the Navy explorer Charles Wilkes emphasized to members of Congress, "can give little idea of the terrors of the bar of the Columbia. All who have seen it have spoken of the wildness of the scene, and the incessant roar of the waters, representing it as one of the most fearful sights that can possibly meet the eye of the sailor." It was in July of

1841 that the *Peacock,* one of several ships of the United States Exploring Expedition under Wilkes' command, ran afoul of the Columbia bar and broke apart in the pounding surf. All lives were saved, but loss of the sloop of war was more than an embarrassment for her commander, Lieutenant William L. Hudson, her one hundred thirty officers and crewmen, and three civilian scientists.

Wilkes used the fate of the *Peacock* to dramatize the importance of Puget Sound as the only truly valuable harbor in the American Northwest. "Nothing can exceed the beauty of these waters, and their safety," and he asserted that no country in the world possessed a waterway equal to it. Because the United States had not yet acquired California, Wilkes's timely warning probably stiffened the resolve of American negotiators who extended the international boundary north of Puget Sound in 1846 and not down the Columbia River as the British preferred. Nonetheless, for many more years the Columbia River remained the primary though always challenging gateway to the sprawling Oregon country for Americans traveling by sea to the region's population centers. It was along its banks and those of the tributary Willamette River that most Euro-American pioneers located their settlements. Even today, two-thirds of Oregon's population is concentrated in the Willamette Valley, which extends a hundred miles from Portland south to Eugene.

In terms of commercial transportation, as late as 1860, when the first stagecoach pounded along the dusty road that linked Portland and the Pacific Northwest with San Francisco, the nation's far corner remained part of the maritime frontier that included Hawaii and California. Because the remote region was bound on one side by the Pacific Ocean and isolated on the other by the Great Basin desert, the snowcapped Rocky Mountains, and the Great Plains, it was in many ways an island that could be reached far more easily by sea than by land, and the Columbia River was its main gateway to and from distant points.

The significance of this historic portal is often overlooked today. It is now the Oregon Trail that is the most celebrated connection between the East and the Pacific Northwest, a bond that was emphasized in the mid

The Columbia Gorge, the water gateway between East and West. Crown Point lies in the foreground, Beacon Rock looms in the distance. Beyond Beacon Rock is modern Bonneville Dam. Courtesy Ralph Lee Hopkins.

Columbia River

As if to symbolize the importance of water in the history of Oregon, a majestic fountain stands on the state capitol grounds in Salem. In the Pacific Northwest, as in few other regions of the United States, water is an abiding presence: fog and rain, glacier and waterfall, irrigation canal and tidal estuary, the Columbia River and Pacific Ocean.

1990s on every new automobile license plate issued in Oregon. There was certainly good reason for that commemoration: the two thousand-mile trek across the West from Missouri to the Willamette Valley was the longest wagon migration undertaken by any sizable number of American settlers (some 53,000 people during the 1840s and 1850s), longer even than to California. In Oregon history, this illustrious trail, covered wagons, and the westering pioneers are comparable to Plymouth Rock, the *Mayflower,* and the Pilgrims in national mythology. But from its origins in early 1843 and until 1864—when steamboat and stagecoach connections at last provided travelers a shortcut west from the overland stage line at Salt Lake City, across the Great Basin desert, and along the Columbia River to Portland— the Oregon Trail remained essentially a private (non-commercial) passage to the Pacific.

For all its deserved fame, the Oregon Trail played no part in the first *regularly scheduled commercial transportation* between Oregon and the rest of the United States. That distinction belongs to the Pacific Mail Steamship Company, which in 1850 commenced three round-trip sailings a month

≈ *William T. C. Stevens rendered this watercolor painting of the Hudson's Bay Company steamer* Beaver, *which in 1836 brought steam power to the remote Pacific Northwest, at Fort Vancouver. Columbia River Maritime Museum copy photo by Steve Eltinge (1982.111.1).*

between San Francisco and Portland. Before this time, ocean-going vessels had called on the Pacific Northwest only at irregular intervals, and with the exception of the aptly named *Beaver* that the Hudson's Bay Company used in the fur trade, none was powered by steam.

During the 1850s, regularly scheduled commercial transportation between Oregon Territory (which then included future Washington and Idaho) and any other part of the United States invariably meant a long and circuitous trip by sea. Leaving Portland or one of the other population outposts of the Willamette Valley, the traveler first sailed west to reach the distant East Coast of North America. That is, passengers, mail, and express traveled down the Columbia River and south along the Pacific Coast to make ship or stagecoach connections in San Francisco. For better or for worse (and for many travelers it was unquestionably for worse), everyone who entered or left Oregon by commercial means had to cross the formidable bar at the Columbia River. Just about the only travelers who managed to avoid it were settlers in scattered villages along Puget Sound and in the Rogue River gold country just north of the Oregon-California border.

A traveler aboard the *Brother Jonathan* in the early 1860s wrote that as the coastal steamship approached the bar, even from a distance "its breakers were imposing: foaming mountains like wild titans roaring and crashing into one another." The captain claimed the passage was actually quite calm. He had sometimes been forced to remain off the bar for days on end before daring to enter its twisting channel. The traveler's journal continues: "During our 'calm' entry our *Brother Jonathan* groaned in every joint, as if the waves wanted to extinguish the fires. A couple of waves met like lovers in a kiss above the deck and my enthusiasm for the romance of those waters cooled considerably." This frightful aquatic gateway seemed to symbolize that nature had bound and isolated the Oregon country.

It was only in mid March 1859 that Oregon learned it had become the nation's thirty-third state, although President James Buchanan had signed the legislation nearly a month earlier on February 14. The welcome news traveled to Oregon in the fastest way possible: by telegraphic dispatch to the

THE LIGHTSHIP *COLUMBIA*

*B*ECAUSE OF THE terrors of the bar, aids to navigation of the Columbia have been an essential part of its history. Today the largest exhibit at the Columbia River Maritime Museum is the bright red lightship *Columbia* (WLV-604). This floating beacon was stationed at the river's mouth from 1951 to 1979, maintaining a service to mariners that dated back to 1892 when the first lightship anchored there. The *Columbia*'s beam was visible for fifteen miles, and through fog her powerful horn sounded a warning that could be heard at least a mile away. The Museum acquired the *Columbia* in 1980. She remains fully operational, occasionally sailing up the river as far as Portland for special events.

end of the wire in Saint Louis, by overland stage to San Francisco, and by the popular steamship *Brother Jonathan* through the Columbia River gateway to reach Portland in just twenty-nine days. The happy tidings continued by horseback to the capitol in Salem.

At first the only practical alternative to overland travel was a tedious ocean voyage around Cape Horn, a distance from coast to coast of eleven to fourteen thousand miles. Life aboard a slow sailing ship was different from, yet rarely any easier than, the journey west to Oregon by wagon. Many a midwesterner chose the shorter land route without hesitation, thus avoiding the unfamiliar and often perilous ordeal of a lengthy ocean voyage. But in settlements along the Atlantic coast, westering Americans took the opposite view: they looked naturally to the sea as the easiest and safest way to reach distant lands. For them a trip by ship avoided the added expense and difficulty of obtaining all the equipment required for a long overland trek,

and it eliminated the risk of attack from hostile Indians (a possibility that haunted the imaginations of travelers on both the Oregon and California trails). Usually it took six to eight months to sail down the eastern seaboard, around South America, and north to the Columbia River.

Whether they arrived by land or sea, all early Oregonians shouldered a heavy burden imposed by time and space. Anyone who survived the hazards of the long journey still had to deal with an overwhelming sense of isolation on the Pacific Coast. During most of the 1840s the nearest post office was located in Weston, Missouri, some two thousand miles distant. If a letter was destined for the States, the sender first had to find someone returning east who would mail it upon reaching Missouri. It was in order to establish mail service with Oregon that the federal government subsidized the Pacific Mail Steamship Company along the coast between Panama and Astoria, the location of the first post office west of the Rocky Mountains. The cost of sending a letter from Astoria "to the United States" was origi-

ABOVE LEFT: *Artist Cleveland Rockwell painted a square rigger at Cape Horn on the Columbia River in the 1880s. At least two separate locations on the lower portion of the waterway are named Cape Horn, probably because the southernmost point of South America was so much a part of the mental geography of early navigators. Columbia River Maritime Museum copy photo by Steve Eltinge (1984.131.1).*

ABOVE: *In May 1995 a modern ocean-going ship heads downriver at a site not far from where Cleveland Rockwell painted his image (see left) of a square rigger at Cape Horn.*

The windswept South Jetty, where the Columbia meets the Pacific Ocean, was constructed as part of an ongoing attempt to tame the currents that regularly changed the channel in this location.

nally forty cents, compared to five cents for letters traveling less than three hundred miles on the East Coast.

Transporting mail, merchandise, and people north along the Pacific Coast from the Golden Gate to the gateway into the Oregon country remained an expensive and difficult ordeal, especially because of the bar at the mouth of the Columbia River. Yet until a final spike was driven at Promontory Summit, Utah, in 1869 to complete the nation's first transcontinental railroad, sailing vessels plying the Cape Horn route formed the vital freight connection between East and West. Travelers by sea after 1849 had the option of taking a shortcut through the jungles of Panama, but while that fifty-mile portage reduced the time of travel to less than a month from coast to coast, it increased a traveler's exposure to diseases like yellow fever, malaria, and cholera. In 1852, the steamer *Philadelphia* was bound for New York City from Panama; she lost one-third of her passengers to disease. The victims included many prominent citizens of the West Coast who were nonetheless unceremoniously heaved overboard in a hapless effort to halt the spread of the plague. Just a year earlier, Oregon's first delegate in Congress, Samuel R. Thurston, died of a tropical fever aboard ship off the West Coast of Mexico.

During the 1850s and 1860s the isthmus of Panama loomed far larger in the transportation geography of average residents of the Pacific Northwest than it does today. The same is true of the place where the Columbia River joins the sea, the hazardous bar that symbolized the many geographical impediments that confined residents of early Oregon within their distant and isolated corner of the United States. In short, while the Columbia River functioned as a pioneer gateway to the West, nature also exacted a toll from all who passed through.

The Astor Column high atop a hill overlooking Astoria and the lower Columbia River depicts scenes from the area's rich history and also affords a panoramic view of the landscape. Courtesy Ralph Lee Hopkins.

CHAPTER TWO

Nature's River

From columbia lake, its source high in the Canadian Rockies, the Great River of the West extends a distance of 1,232 miles to reach the Pacific Ocean; together with its many tributary waterways the Columbia drains an area of 258,000 square miles. Flowing into the Columbia just north of the Canadian border is the Pend Oreille River, which adds water from northern Idaho and western Montana. The Columbia's largest and longest tributary, the Snake River, joins it near Pasco. From there the channel of the expanding waterway twists south through Wallula Gap and then turns abruptly west.

Originating a thousand miles east, near Yellowstone Park, the Snake is itself a major river of the United States. After cutting through lava plains and the "famous potatoes" country of southern Idaho, where a portion of its water irrigates six million acres of farmland, the Snake plunges into Hells Canyon, the deepest gorge in North America. The Deschutes and John Day rivers flow into the Columbia east of the Cascades after draining the sparsely populated landscape of central Oregon. About a hundred miles from sea, the waters of the Willamette River, having served the needs of Portland, Salem, and Eugene, join the Columbia's massive flow. This brief listing by no means accounts for all of the river's many tributaries.

➤ OPPOSITE: *Along the Columbia River near The Dalles, Oregon, is where dense forests west of the Cascades give way to dry grasslands that typify the landscape east of the range.*

➤ ABOVE: *In the dry country of eastern Washington are the Twin Captains or Twin Sisters, a basalt formation easily visible from the Columbia River in western Walla Walla County. Lewis and Clark described this landmark on their way west in 1805.*

Source of the river: Columbia Lake in the Rocky Mountains of southeastern British Columbia.

The Columbia River itself flows through four mountain ranges, pours more water into the ocean than any other rivers in North America except for the Saint Lawrence, Mississippi, and Mackenzie, and exceeds every waterway on the continent in the generation of hydroelectric power. In fact, its waters if fully harnessed would provide an estimated forty percent of the nation's total hydroelectric power, but any proposal to build another dam

20

Columbia River

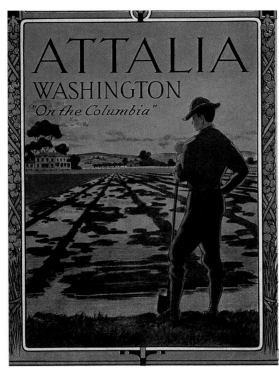

on the Columbia River would probably generate far more public controversy than electricity. Except for a fifty-mile stretch of free-flowing river along the Hanford Nuclear Reservation in central Washington, the Columbia has already been engineered into a chain of lakes that extends all the way from Bonneville Dam to just south of the Canadian border. Through a series of eight massive locks—including the world's deepest in John Day Dam—towboats and barges can climb the Columbia and Snake rivers to reach Idaho's only seaport, Lewiston, which is located four hundred sixty-five miles inland and more than seven hundred feet above sea level.

Nature lavished her favors on the Columbia River, and not just in terms of water for irrigation or to power the massive turbines that generate electricity. Vaporous clouds of mist and rain sweep in from the Pacific Ocean to nurture the dense forests of Douglas fir and Sitka spruce that once lined both banks of the lower Columbia. These forests caused one

ABOVE LEFT: *Water from the Columbia River and its various tributaries irrigates crops in many different parts of Oregon, Washington, Idaho, and Montana. This image is of sprinklers near Sisters, Oregon, in the high desert watershed of the Deschutes River, which enters the Columbia above today's The Dalles Dam.*

ABOVE: *The magic of irrigation. The cover image of an early twentieth century promotional brochure advertises the irrigated oasis of Attalia in western Walla Walla County near the confluence of the Columbia and Snake rivers. Courtesy Oregon Historical Society.*

commentator to quip in 1874, "Astoria, however, means to grow. It has already a large hotel, which the timber has crowded down against the tide-washed flats; a saw-mill which is sawing away for dear life, because if it stopped the forest would push it into the river, on whose brink it has courageously effected lodgement."

In the river itself swam unbelievable numbers of fish. "The salmon commence entering the Columbia and its tributaries about the 1st of April in such numberless millions," wrote sportsman and journalist John Mortimer Murphy in the late 1870s. Observing their spawning behavior he noted "that the water fairly boils with them, and by the middle of the month they are so dense that they crowd each other ashore, and myriads die from exhaustion."

LEFT: *The evergreen wilderness of the Columbia Gorge.*

BELOW: *These artifacts in the woods below Bonneville Dam recall the days when railroads portaged passengers and freight around the upper and lower Cascades, two rapids now hidden by waters impounded by the dam.*

BELOW BOTTOM: *The Pacific Crest Trail crosses the Columbia River at Cascade Locks.*

COLUMBIA RIVER GORGE NATIONAL SCENIC AREA

$\mathcal{N}$ATURE SEEMS ESPECIALLY generous along the ninety-mile stretch of river known as the Columbia Gorge, where the waterway slices through the Cascade Range to link the wet and dry sides of the Pacific Northwest. Tangled undergrowth and moisture-loving, moss-festooned forest giants like the Sitka spruce and Douglas fir thrive in the damp climate west of the Cascades before giving way to ponderosa pines on the eastern slopes and eventually to the grasses and sagebrush that survive where annual rainfall averages ten inches or less.

To most early travelers, the dramatic transition from wet to dry country and the juxtaposition of water and mountains formed a landscape panorama unsurpassed on the continent. Aboard a steamboat in the 1860s one viewer commented, "The admirers of mountain scenery will be constantly on the deck, admiring the ever varying battlements of basalt which shoot up several thousand feet high on either side. To gaze on them was really a perpetual feast to all of us." Another early-day commentator declared the scenery grander than that seen along the palisades of the Hudson River, a favorite haunt of the nation's early artists.

For most travelers, the crown jewel of the Columbia Gorge was (and is) Multnomah Falls, which drops sixty-two stories

down the face of Larch Mountain (a distance of about 620 feet). John Mortimer Murphy once described the nation's second highest waterfall as a "ribbon of white" that long before it reached its "craggy bed or the heavy forests far beneath" had dissolved into "snowy drops of spray, which were whirled in every direction by the lightest zephyrs. After uniting below they plowed their way in a tortuous course through moss-lined banks and tangled shrubbery until they made their final leap into the Columbia in a broad and thin sheet of silvery water." Even Murphy's purple prose could not do full justice to the landscape of the Columbia Gorge, and that is probably one reason why it remains such a favorite site for nature photographers who relish the challenge of capturing its many moods on film.

The mountain-and-water landscape between Troutdale and The Dalles is so

One of many waterfalls that adds beauty and drama to the Columbia Gorge. Courtesy Ralph Lee Hopkins.

awe-inspiring that in 1986 Congress designated it the Columbia River Gorge National Scenic Area, to be managed by the United States Forest Service. Opponents, who feared that communities hemmed in by the preserve would become ghost towns, preferred development to aesthetics. President Ronald Reagan signed the bill nonetheless.

The occasional low clouds and mist that shroud distant promontories only heighten the Gorge's appeal for romantics who are inclined to append words like "brooding" and "mysterious" to the landscape. Rand McNally's 1991 *Road Atlas* named the portion of Interstate 84 through the Gorge one of America's eight "Top Scenic Routes." No other stretch of superhighway was included among this most select list of "blue highways."

Today the Columbia Gorge attracts as many as five million visitors a year. Most people come to contemplate the scenery and enjoy the many recreational opportunities the valley and its ramparts afford. But the area is also rich in history. The Columbia Gorge probably witnessed more key events in the region's transportation history than any comparable site. Not many of the "first" or "most significant" developments are obvious today from the river or nearby Interstate 84; some are not even commemorated with roadside markers. Yet in the Gorge workmen hammered into place the wooden tracks of a crude portage line in 1851. The region's first railway ran a short distance along the Washington bank of the river and was designed to hasten passengers and freight around the dangerous stretch of white water known as the Cascades. Called the Cascades Railroad, it was a primitive affair that used mules to pull flatcars along six-inch square wooden rails topped with strap iron. For 75 cents, 100 pounds of "emigrant effects" could be portaged around the rapids. Over its tracks rumbled trains of four or five cars pulled by horses and mules.

Still preserved and on display in the town of Cascade Locks is the Oregon Pony, which puffed its way to fame in 1862 as the first steam locomotive in the Pacific Northwest. Close by are the remains of the old locks themselves, now mainly a haunt of fishermen, but when completed in 1896, they at last opened the river to steamboat traffic between Portland and The Dalles. The Cascade Locks Marine Park is a National Historic Site.

Multnomah Falls, in the heart of the Columbia River Gorge National Scenic Area, is Oregon's most visited tourist attraction. Columbia River Maritime Museum photo by Steve Eltinge.

CAUGHT IN SALT WATER AND CANNED IMMEDIATELY AFTER BEING CAUGHT

DIRECTIONS
OPEN ON OUTER EDGE NEAR THE TOP SO FISH WILL COME OUT WHOLE. TO SERVE HOT PLACE CAN IN BOILING WATER FOR TWENTY MINUTES

EMPTY CONTENTS OF CAN AS SOON AS OPENED.

Columbia River SALMON PACKED AT ASTORIA, OREGON.

CHEF BRAND

GEO. W. SANBORN, AGENT. ASTORIA, ✳ OREGON.

ABOVE: *A colorful label for Columbia River salmon packed at Astoria is one of hundreds once used by dozens of canneries on the lower Columbia. Courtesy Columbia River Maritime Museum (1984.46.8).*

OPPOSITE: *The rain-washed waterfront of modern Astoria. Its name evokes the fur-trade era in Pacific Northwest history, though in more recent times it was synonymous with fishing, canning, and lumbering.*

The salmon of the Columbia River were a major source of food and an object of trade for the many different Indian tribes who lived along the river's banks—even as the waterway itself served as an avenue of trade and commerce and knitted together the Pacific Northwest well before the coming of Euro-American pioneers. For Indian peoples as well as for the new-comers, the Columbia counteracted the divisive influence of mountains, especially the Cascade Range, a wall breached only by the spectacular Columbia Gorge and one other river, the Klamath, in southern Oregon. Taking greatest advantage of the geography of the Columbia River were the Chinookan peoples—the Clatsops, Cathlamets, Skilloots, and others whose homeland lay along the lower Columbia River—who occupied a strategic position as middlemen in the trade between Indians to the north and south and between those of the coast and the interior. Long-distance trade was common: for example, through Chinookan traders, prized shells from the west coast of Vancouver Island reached Indians of the interior.

Perhaps the single most important intertribal gathering in the Pacific

OPPOSITE: *Native fishermen at Celilo Falls, above The Dalles, in October 1933. Courtesy Oregon Historical Society.*

LEFT: *Remnants of a native village below The Dalles Dam, where slack water inundated once-popular fisheries there and at Celilo Falls farther upriver.*

Northwest took place at the Grand Dalles of the Columbia River, where native peoples of the coast met regularly with dwellers of the vast Columbia Plateau. Here was the cosmopolitan center of the region's Indian life, the site of great month-long trade fairs analogous to those held in medieval Europe; it was a time for trading, dancing, ceremonial displays, games, gambling, and even marriages. The Wishrams and Wascos sometimes hosted several thousand visitors who came to trade items from the interior, such as bison robes, for those from the coast: dried salmon, canoes, marine shells and shell beads, and fish oil. The development of complex patterns of exchange enabled Indian trade goods from the Pacific Northwest to reach as far as Alaska, southern California, and even Missouri long before the coming of Euro-Americans.

What is perhaps most remarkable about this intertribal gathering is that native peoples of the Pacific Northwest spoke a bewildering variety of languages and dialects that were as mutually unintelligible as English and Japanese. To facilitate communication among Indians as well as with the

 *A storm in 1995 near Pendleton, Oregon, intensifies the color of the spring landscape of the Columbia Plateau, which in late summer and fall is an important source of the grain sent downriver to Portland.*

Euro-Americans, the Chinook jargon emerged as a common tongue. A simply structured hybrid language that by the 1830s had expanded to include about seven hundred words of Indian, English, and French origin, and was augmented by signs, the Chinook jargon proved remarkably adaptable to embracing additional words to describe new trade goods. But it was poorly suited to Euro-American attempts to explain complex matters like land holding and religion. One unhappy result of a cultural gulf that could not be bridged by language was a series of treaties negotiated between Whites and Indians, the meanings of which are still a matter of legal dispute.

It is worth noting here that the Chinook word for citizens of the United States was "Boston," which accurately reflects the New England dominance of America's maritime frontier on the North Pacific Coast. And with the coming of the "Bostons" and the rival "King George Men," and their new Euro-American way of envisioning the Columbia as a source of personal and national wealth, nature's river was changed forever.

Snowmelt in the Cascade Mountains of Washington, a transportation barrier breached only by the Columbia River and the Klamath River of southern Oregon.

CHAPTER THREE

ENVISIONING THE COLUMBIA RIVER

AMONG THE MANY islands of the Columbia River are several called *Memaloose.* The most important one is located between The Dalles and Hood River. The word in the Chinook jargon means "death" or "dead" and derives from the fact that Native Americans used these islands as burial grounds. *Memaloose* reminds us that virtually every place name on the river has a story behind it: some of these are biographical, others are capsule histories. Collectively they hint at the river's many overlapping historical landscapes, because alongside the numerous Native American names—such as Washougal, Klickitat, and Umatilla—there are also places called Astoria, Vancouver, Rainier, St. Helens, and Hood River.

The name "John Day River" tells of an American fur trader who headed west to help establish Fort Astoria but became lost. Before his companions found him wandering in a daze along the Columbia River, local Indians had stripped him of his clothes and left him stranded without even a flint to build a fire. Regardless of the stories they tell, many of these place names remind us of the early Euro-American presence in the Pacific Northwest and the era of the fur trade, the first big business on the Columbia River.

It was difficult for European explorers in the 1700s even to envision the

OPPOSITE: *Astoria is where the last highway bridge crosses the Columbia River before the broad waterway reaches the sea.*

ABOVE: *Early morning river traffic below John Day Dam in November 1996.*

possibility of the Columbia River. Long after most of the world's temperate coastlines had been explored, it still had no place on their maps or in their thinking. In 1775, while returning from a voyage that had probed as far north as present-day southeastern Alaska, the Spanish explorer Bruno de Heceta (or Hezeta) detected a powerful current pushing against his ship, the *Santiago,* and this led him to speculate that "it may be the mouth of some great river or some passage to another sea." But because his men were so weak from scurvy, Heceta hesitated to cross the great river's treacherous bar and instead hurried south to Monterey and then on to his base in Mexico. Because of the competitive nature of international exploration at the time, the Spanish government kept his findings secret. Credit for the important discovery thus goes to an American merchant captain, Robert Gray, who in May 1792 sailed into the Columbia and confirmed what Heceta had noticed.

Gray's ship, the *Columbia Rediviva,* had earlier become the first United States vessel to circumnavigate the globe when she returned to Boston harbor in 1790. A swarm of American fur traders and whalers soon followed

Gray's lead, commencing the long voyage from New England ports, rounding Cape Horn, and fanning out into all parts of the Pacific, most notably China, in search of markets to replace those lost when the United States gained its independence from Great Britain.

Gray was a merchant seaman who reached North Pacific waters well after the European empires of Great Britain, Spain, Russia, and even France had explored the numerous bays and inlets and (except for France) established elaborate trade networks with native peoples. Like latecomers to any frontier, he found the field of opportunity considerably narrowed. But undiscouraged, he sought to trade for the valuable pelts of fur-bearing animals like the sea otter. In the process, Gray entered the harbor on the coast of Washington that bears his name and the great river he named for his ship. His men spent nine days in the river and charted its lower reaches. Though Gray himself never returned to the remote Columbia country, he laid the foundation for a United States claim to the area. He also deposited a rough chart of the lower river with his friend Bodega y Quadra, the Spanish governor at Nootka on Vancouver Island, and thereby duly notified European powers of the American discovery.

Following in Gray's historical wake, George Vancouver's British expedition reached the mouth of the Columbia in October 1792. His lieutenant, William Broughton, surveyed a hundred miles up the river to a site near present-day Vancouver, Washington, and made the first detailed chart of the lower waterway. Broughton contended that Gray never actually entered the river itself but only the sound at its mouth. That assertion was the basis for a British claim to the

Low hanging clouds typify the wet weather encountered by Lewis and Clark as they searched for a suitable campsite near the mouth of the river.

Columbia, although when Broughton's charts were published in 1798 they continued the name Gray gave to the river. Curiously, Gray's original chart was later found among Vancouver's papers.

The next major opportunity for Americans to envision the Columbia River by means of charts, maps, and descriptive prose came in the fall of 1805, when members of the Lewis and Clark expedition finally reached the waterway after a harrowing ordeal in the snows of the Bitterroot Mountains of what is now central Idaho. After entrusting their horses to the Nez Perce Indians and constructing five dugout canoes on a riverbank near future Orofino, Idaho, the explorers paddled down the Clearwater, Snake, and Columbia rivers. When on November 7, 1805, the Corps of

Discovery neared the long-sought waters of the Pacific, William Clark rejoiced in his notebook, "Great joy in camp we are in *View* of the Ocian, this great Pacific Octean which we been So long anxious to See. and the roreing or noise made by the waves brakeing on the rockey Shores (as I suppose) may be heard distinctly."

So intent was Clark on reaching his long-sought goal that his imagination apparently got the best of him, for he mistook an estuary of the Columbia River for the Pacific Ocean, which the expedition did not reach until a few days later. After ten storm-plagued days in camp on the north shore, the expedition relocated across the river to a more favorable site. On December 8, the men began to build a small stockade on the Netul (now Lewis and Clark River); they named it Fort Clatsop for the nearest Indian tribe.

After enduring an exceedingly damp and disagreeable winter (only twelve days were free of rain) and failing to secure a hoped-for ship home, the Lewis and Clark expedition returned east up the Columbia River on March 23, 1806. Once more they faced the daunting prospect of crossing the

A modern recreation of Fort Clatsop, near Astoria, recalls where members of the Lewis and Clark expedition spent the soggy winter of 1805–1806.

Bitterroot Mountains, where deep snow blocked their way until late June. Finally, on September 23, 1806, they returned to Saint Louis, where they were greeted with great rejoicing.

Lewis and Clark accomplished much more than simply adding a noteworthy chapter to the history of exploration. Their journals, which rank among the treasures of the nation's written history, contain descriptive prose, drawings, and detailed maps that added greatly to popular knowledge about terrain, native peoples, and the flora and fauna of the West. There was far more to envisioning the Columbia country than exploring, mapping, and describing it, however. The journals of Lewis and Clark, together with their numerous specimens and artifacts, revealed a land rich in beaver and other fur-bearing animals. This information lured a generation of trappers and traders west to exploit the region's vast fur resources, first primarily the sea otters that lived near the river's mouth and then the beavers that lived along the mountain streams and lakes farther inland.

There was considerable money to be made in the fur trade. The hat-making industry alone required a hundred thousand beaver pelts each year to satisfy demand—until the beavers were depleted and the hats went out

THE VOYAGE OF THE *TONQUIN*

⸻

To turn his dream into reality, Astor dispatched two expeditions, one by land and another by sea, to the North Pacific coast. The Astorians heading overland from Saint Louis meandered needlessly and endured great hunger, thirst, sickness, death, and even madness, as the fate of John Day attests. Seagoing members of Astor's enterprise fared no better. Laden with thirty-three young Scots and Canadians, trade goods, and materials to erect a fortified post, the three hundred-ton ship *Tonquin* sailed from New York City in September 1810 and made her way around Cape Horn to the Columbia River.

The eight-month, 22,000 mile voyage was an ill-starred affair, filled with bickering and feuding between the bad-tempered Captain Jonathan Thorn on one side and his crew and passengers on the other. As they prepared to enter the Columbia River, Thorn's stubbornness cost eight crewmen their lives when he ordered them out in small boats to seek a passable channel through the treacherous waters of the bar. "Farewell my friends, we will perhaps meet again in the next world," was one departing officer's tragically accurate prediction of his fate. The needless deaths cast a pall over the entire enterprise as the ship battled its way to a protected cove on the south bank of the river. There, in late March 1811, passengers and supplies were unloaded and Fort Astoria took shape.

Astor hoped to use the *Tonquin* to transport furs to China, but that was not to be. What actually happened to the *Tonquin* after she left Astoria to trade with the inhabitants of Nootka Sound may never be known, but according to the ship's native interpreter, who escaped harm, the tyrannical Captain Thorn so antagonized the Indians—on one occasion rubbing a headman's face with a fur in a trade dispute—that they rushed aboard the vessel, overwhelmed the crew of twenty-three to twenty-six hands, and proceeded to kill every one. However, a few sailors reached the hold where they touched off several tons of black powder, blowing themselves, nearly two hundred Nootkas, and Astor's little ship of horrors to bits.

of style. From the 1780s to the 1840s the fur trade remained the principal economic activity in the Pacific Northwest. So great were the profits to be made from selling the warm and fashionable furs that pelts were prized as "soft gold," and it was in pursuit of this wealth that John Jacob Astor added his name to the river's historical landscape (and later, after investing in New York City real estate, became America's first millionaire).

Astor, a businessman whose interest in the Pacific Northwest was stimulated by reports of the region's natural wealth, laid plans for a vast new business empire. A stout, arrogant immigrant who came to the United States from Germany in 1784, he had been involved in the fur trade of the upper Great Lakes. It was early information from Lewis and Clark that seemed to crystallize his evolving plan for the Pacific coast. After learning about the "soft gold" of the far West, he organized the Pacific Fur Company in 1810 to tap the riches of the Oregon country on a grand scale, a move made in defiance of British claims to the area.

Astor supplied money for the new enterprise while a group of Canadians and Americans served as partners and managed operations in the field. From a post he proposed to build near the mouth of the Columbia River, his traders and trappers would fan out across the Northwest to collect furs for markets in China. Astor also viewed his Pacific Fur Company as an American response to British-Canadian challengers. But things did not work out as he had hoped. Even getting his base established near the mouth of the Columbia River proved a daunting task.

From their base near the mouth of the Columbia, the Astorians headed out in several directions to explore and exploit the fur resources of the Northwest. They built Fort Okanogan (the first American structure in the future state of Washington) and Fort Spokane and posts on the Clearwater and Boise rivers. A seven-man party led by Robert Stuart returned overland from Fort Astoria to New York in mid 1812 and located, quite by accident, an easy crossing over the Continental Divide that had eluded Lewis and Clark. By traveling slightly south of the Astorians' original route west, the Stuart party discovered South Pass, a broad and gentle route through

OPPOSITE: *The afternoon shadow of Beacon Rock reaches upriver toward Bonneville Dam.*

the Rockies and the key geographic feature that made the future Oregon Trail possible.

British and American fur traders engaged in a lively competition in the Oregon country that ended prematurely with the outbreak of the War of 1812. News of the conflict reached Astoria early in 1813, and after months of indecision, the Americans agreed under duress to sell out to their British competitors at a substantial loss. Although the Astorians' presence in the Pacific Northwest was brief, they nonetheless proved highly significant in bolstering a future United States claim to the area. Yet during the next three decades it was a British and Canadian fur enterprise that prevailed in the sprawling Oregon country, notably the Hudson's Bay Company.

Chartered by King Charles II in 1670 (and thus of such ancient lineage that some humorists claimed its initials stood for "Here Before Christ"), the Governor and Company of Adventurers of England Trading into Hudson's Bay dominated the Columbia country from the early 1820s until the mid 1840s. During most of those years, Fort Vancouver (now in Vancouver, Washington) functioned as the regional nerve center of a vast and complex commercial system based not only on furs, but also on a lively trade in deer hides, prized shells, gold dust, and the various products of farm, forest, and stream. Those company employees who were not active in the fur trade were to remain busily engaged in farming, fishing, or some other profitable work. Such diversification made grain, beef, butter, fish, and wood from the Columbia River available for sale in foreign markets such as Russian Alaska, thus lessening the company's dependency on fur profits.

On the broad, fertile plain that extended along the north bank of the Columbia River arose a small, almost self-sufficient European community that included a hospital, school, several churches, thirty to fifty small houses where employees lived with their Indian wives, storehouses for furs, trading goods, and grain, and workshops where artisans and laborers engaged in blacksmithing, carpentry, barrel making, and other crafts. Trade routes extended inland from Fort Vancouver's bustling wharves to the mountain headwaters of the Columbia River and its major tributaries, up the coast to Russian Alaska, and across the Pacific to Asian markets. An overland canoe

Tracks of the Oregon Railway and Navigation Company thread their way through the Pillars of Hercules, a natural formation on the western edge of the Oregon side of the Columbia Gorge. Lithograph from L. Samuel's Columbia River Illustrated *(Portland, 1882); courtesy Columbia River Maritime Museum (1978.83).*

route even reached across North America to connect the Columbia and Saint Lawrence rivers.

On a typical journey to one of the upriver trading posts in the early 1840s, the men of the Hudson's Bay Company used special wooden bateaux renowned for their great strength and buoyancy. Each of these vessels usually carried eight or nine crewmen and about three tons of freight packed into ninety-pound bales of groceries, clothing, flour, powder, bullets, and other supplies. The usual flotilla consisted of nine boats that were rowed by sixty voyageurs—mostly French Canadians and some Iroquois Indians (occasionally accompanied by their wives)—who used heavy oars and sometimes a square sail to muscle their way upriver against the swift current.

The first obstacle encountered was the Cascades, where each of two portages required that hundreds of pounds of goods be unloaded and loaded again. "To a stranger, unacquainted with navigation of this river, the management of these boatmen becomes a source of wonder; for it is surprising how they can succeed in surmounting such rapids at all as the Cascades." Men pulled their empty boats through the foaming waters while the loads were "secured on the back of a voyageur by a band which passes around the forehead and under and over the bale; he squats down, adjusts his load, and rises with ninety pounds on his back; another places ninety

— *A replica of Chief Concomly's canoe rests atop Coxcomb Hill near Astoria. He hosted the explorers Lewis and Clark on the lower Columbia River in 1805.*

pounds more on the top, and off he trots, half bent, to the end of the portage," observed Joseph Drayton, an artist who accompanied the Wilkes Expedition of the early 1840s.

An officer of the Hudson's Bay Company told Drayton that he had seen a voyageur carry "six packages of ninety pounds on his back (five hundred and forty pounds); but it was for a wager, and the distance was not more than one hundred yards. The voyageurs in general have not the appearance of being very strong men. At these portages, the Indians assist for a small present of tobacco. The boats seldom escape injury in passing; and in consequence of that which they received on this occasion, the party was detained the rest of the day repairing damages." Waters impounded by Bonneville Dam have covered this historic landscape since 1937.

Another, even more difficult passage was located at the Grand Dalles, where the whole river seemed to be turned on edge. On the morning of July 4, Drayton observed in amazement as the voyageurs began the mile-long portage.

It is very rugged, and the weather being exceedingly warm, many of the Indians were employed to transport articles on their horses, of which they have a large number. It required seventy men to transport the boats, which were carried over bottom upwards, the gunwale resting on the men's shoulders. By night all was safely transported, the boats newly gummed, and the encampment formed on a sandy beach. The sand, in consequence of the high wind, was blown about in great quantities, and every body and thing was literally covered with it.

Ahead a few miles more were the Chutes (or Celilo Falls) where they made yet another portage. From here they pulled their boats as far as the John Day River because the Columbia was so filled with boulders. Today both the Grand Dalles and Celilo Falls lie beneath slack water created by The Dalles Dam in 1957.

Not only was the fur trade the Pacific Northwest's first big business, it also generated an extensive fund of geographic information that helped residents of distant parts of the world better envision the region. During the first third of the nineteenth century, explorers, together with fur traders and trappers, roamed the Pacific Northwest, combining geographic information acquired from Native American informants with first-hand observations. Descriptions of the Columbia country by Lewis and Clark were vivid enough, but they took no artist with them to the Pacific. In fact, for another forty years it was mainly through maps and verbal descriptions that Americans became acquainted with the Columbia River.

Most people treated this growing body of information in terms of how to make money, win souls, or establish homes in the Pacific Northwest. Seeing the Great River of the West primarily in terms of aesthetic pleasure was not easy. But beginning in the 1840s, a series of vivid paintings captured the beauty of the Columbia country as never before. Joseph Drayton of the Wilkes Expedition made sketches and paintings for a lengthy report published in 1845, but it was the gifted Canadian artist Paul Kane who really captured the full magnificence of the Columbia River in his paintings. During

The Dalles today. The Columbia River lies at its doorstep, and Mount Hood, Oregon's highest peak, provides a dramatic backdrop.

Envisioning the Columbia River

the 1850s, artists of the Pacific Railroad Survey that Congress funded to explore suitable routes to the West Coast added to the growing body of visual information about the Columbia River. Finally, in the 1860s, California photographer Carleton Watkins captured vivid images of humans and nature along the waterway. Both professional and amateur photographers have followed in his steps ever since. Like Watkins, most of them used their cameras to emphasize aesthetic aspects of the river landscape.

Meanwhile, by the 1860s the prevailing vision fixated on how best to coin money from nature's abundance on the Columbia. The focus shifted from the once lucrative fur trade to fishing and canning as salmon replaced the beaver and sea otter as important sources of riches. Five varieties of salmon were caught along the entire Pacific watershed, especially in the lower Columbia River. Salmon are anadromous; that is, they originate in fresh water but spend most of their adult life in the ocean, ranging across thousands of miles. After approximately five years they return home to spawn, sometimes in remote tributaries of the Columbia River a thousand miles or more from the sea, although in recent decades the building of dams has narrowed the fish's inland range. The image of millions of salmon returning upstream, driven by some mysterious instinct to leap rapids and

low waterfalls, caused salmon to become as closely identified with the wild Northwest as cod were with New England.

The modern salmon industry on the Columbia dated from 1866 when two brothers, William and George Hume, opened a small cannery on the lower river. Profits were spectacular because canned salmon was popular in the East, Great Britain, and other areas as a cheap but nourishing working-class food. From that modest beginning, more than fifty canneries dotted the banks of the lower Columbia River and its tributaries by 1883, and Astoria, with twenty-five canneries, became the heart of the industry. For a time it was Oregon's second largest city. The Columbia River salmon catch peaked in 1895 with 635,000 cases (each holding 48 one-pound cans), by which time the industry had also become quite large on Puget Sound.

Fishermen were predominantly Scandinavians and Finns who logged or farmed in the off-season. Many cannery workers were Chinese. Canning was at first a slow, messy business with individual tins requiring careful soldering by hand. Beginning in 1905, however, a revolutionary machine called the Iron Chink (with unselfconscious racism) dramatically thinned the ranks of cannery workers by doing the work of fifty men. By means of rotating knives and brushes, this machine automatically decapitated and

Fishing nets were stretched for drying and repair at the Columbia River Packers' Association Sanborn-Cutting Company plant on Astoria's waterfront. Courtesy Columbia River Maritime Museum (1978.84).

A historic image of a fishwheel, one of many different designs located along the middle and lower Columbia until they were outlawed during the late 1920s and early 1930s. Lithograph from L. Samuel's Columbia River Illustrated (Portland, 1882); courtesy Columbia River Maritime Museum (1978.83).

cleaned fish at the rate of one per second. Another change occurred at the turn of the century when numerous small canneries formed cooperatives such as the Columbia River Packers' Association to market their products more efficiently and to stabilize profits.

Cutthroat competition and unsound practices, like stringing traps and nets across river mouths so that few adult fish survived to spawn, characterized commercial fishing almost from the beginning. At times such an armada of fishing craft jammed the lower Columbia that it seemed a person could walk across the river on their decks. In the late 1880s the Army Corps of Engineers inventoried nearly three million feet of nets and seines in the river, along with numerous fish wheels. This mass of equipment apparently was great enough to slow the flow of the mighty Columbia.

Early on, cannery operators on the Columbia River expressed concern about yearly fluctuations in salmon runs. The Washington legislature declared a closed season in 1877; Oregon responded the following year with two weak conservation measures, one regulating the size of openings in gill nets to allow smaller fish to escape, the other prohibiting fishing during certain hours of the week. Neither Oregon nor Washington vigorously enforced their early conservation measures. Over the decades a bewildering accretion of laws and regulations—such as those outlawing traps, explosives, and drugs—attempted to protect commercial fishermen from themselves. Quite simply, they possessed technology too efficient to insure their

WHEELS OF FORTUNE

⁓

LOATING SALMON WHEELS were once a common sight in the Columbia Gorge, where they efficiently and relentlessly scooped tons of fish from the river. The first fishwheel on the Columbia dated from 1879; twenty years later, seventy-six were in operation. The last ones stopped turning only in 1934 after the state of Washington outlawed them. Rudyard Kipling left a vivid description of their operation in 1889:

> "You'll see the salmon-wheels 'fore long," said a man who lived "way back on the Washoogle," and whose hat was spangled with trout flies. "Those Chinook salmon never rise to fly. The canneries take them by the wheel." At the next bend we sighted a wheel—an infernal arrangement of wire gauze compartments worked by the current and moved out from a barge in shore to scoop up the salmon as he races up the river. California swore long and fluently at the sight, and more fluently when he was told of the weight of a good night's catch—some thousands of pounds. Think of the black and bloody murder of it. But you out yonder insist on buying tinned salmon, and the canneries cannot live by letting down lines.

industry's long-term survival without some form of regulation or cooperation.

Envisioning the Columbia River as a resource to exploit came naturally to Euro-Americans after their first encounters with the waterway. Respecting its superabundant natural resources as finite and requiring conservation to make them available to future generations proved far more difficult. Well before that happened, a host of new technologies would dramatically transform the Great River of the West in ways scarcely imaginable a century and a half ago.

OPPOSITE: *A survivor from a once major industry, this seafood processing plant is located at Ilwaco, Washington, on historic Bakers Bay near the mouth of the Columbia River.*

BELOW: *Haul seining at Kaboth Sands near Astoria in 1914. Courtesy Columbia River Maritime Museum (1964.9.23).*

CHAPTER FOUR

GREAT RIVER OF THE WEST

SALMON WHEELS AND paddle wheels: one machine used the current of the Columbia, harnessing power to harvest tons of fish; the other used steam, enabling the boat to overcome the river's powerful current. As different as they were, neither machine could exist apart from the river. The new age of steam dawned in the Pacific Northwest on May 16, 1836, when the *Beaver,* a diminutive side-wheeler built on the Thames near London and purchased by the Hudson's Bay Company, first fired up her boilers at Fort Vancouver. The British fur monopoly intended the *Beaver* to be a working vessel, a small cog in a large and complex economic machine that embraced dozens of trading posts and farms, several thousand employees, and operations that extended along the Pacific Coast from Spanish California to Russian Alaska. The company's primary interest was the pursuit of profits from furs, but a few excursions beforehand seemed an appropriate way to celebrate the promise of steam power.

Guests of the Hudson's Bay Company boarded the *Beaver* on June 14 for a day-long cruise down the Columbia River from Fort Vancouver into the much narrower Multnomah channel of the Willamette River, around low-lying Sauvie Island and into the main channel, then back to the Columbia and the company's district headquarters. For the most part the

OPPOSITE: She Who Watches *is an example of Native American rock art. This piece is in Washington's Horsethief Lake State Park, located a short distance upriver and on the opposite side from The Dalles. Courtesy Ralph Lee Hopkins.*

ABOVE: *Fall colors in the Columbia River Gorge in November 1998.*

Offering quite a contrast to the days of steam on the river, a tugboat pushes its load of barges upriver through scenic Wallula Gap.

Cargo containers, some of them headed to Japan with frozen French fries from southern Idaho, travel downriver through the locks at The Dalles Dam. They will be loaded aboard ocean-going ships in the Portland-Vancouver area.

passengers must have seen only trees and water, for signs of human habitation were few. Among the lighthearted group that pleasant summer day was the missionary Samuel Parker, for whom the novelty of a steamboat ride on the Great River of the West "awakened a train of prospective reflections upon the probable changes, which would take place in these remote regions, in a very few years." For Parker and other guests the *Beaver* represented a "forerunner of commerce and business. The animation which prevailed was often suspended, while we conversed of coming days, when with civilized men, all the rapid improvements in the arts of life, should be introduced over this new world, and when cities and villages shall spring up on the west, as they are springing up on the east of the great mountains, and a new empire be added to the kingdoms of the earth."

The excursionists aboard the *Beaver* in 1836 were better prophets than they knew. Travelers who retraced that historic voyage today would begin at the eastern edge of the modern city of Vancouver, Washington (population 46,380), where a multi-lane highway, airfield, and railroad embankment isolate the National Park Service's re-created Fort Vancouver from the Columbia River that was once its lifeline. Heading downriver, the modern excursionists would pass several industrial complexes, one for shipping grain to Asia and another where the first aluminum plant in the Pacific Northwest was built in 1940. Turning southeast into the still heavily forested Multnomah channel, they would see a large wood products plant at Saint Helens, Oregon.

Sauvie Island retains a bucolic appearance, but farther up the serpentine channel a houseboat suburb of Portland crowds both sides of the waterway. Along the main part of the Willamette, dry docks, oil storage facilities, warehouses, and large ships line the modern channel all the way to Portland, a city of more than half a million people by the late 1990s. When the *Beaver* first steamed along the Willamette River, Portland did not exist (and would not for another nine years). In fact, apart from fur traders and trappers and several missionaries, of whom Samuel Parker was the vanguard, the Euro-American presence in the Pacific Northwest was negligible. Parker's 1836 excursion aboard the *Beaver* occurred almost midway through a century bracketed by the first sustained contact between Europe and the Pacific Northwest in the early 1780s and the completion of a northern transcontinental railroad in 1883 that closely linked the region to the Midwest and East Coast for the first time.

Less than a week after the historic excursion, Parker took passage aboard the *Beaver* to Fort George (the site of modern Astoria), where a few days later he transferred to a barque bound for the Hawaiian Islands.

Pleasure boaters pass the working waterfront along the lower Willamette River.

This massive guillotine gate is at John Day Dam, the location of what is supposedly the deepest lock chamber in the world at 113 feet.

Parker was pleased to reach Honolulu only sixteen days later; in mid-December he sailed back to the East Coast. His ship followed the usual route around South America and reached New London the following May in 1837. Although he prepared the way for several missionary couples to journey to the Pacific Northwest, Parker himself never returned.

Neither did the *Beaver* return to the Columbia River or Fort Vancouver. The pioneer steam vessel kept busy serving the needs of the Hudson's Bay Company along the North Pacific coast to Alaska and had no time for any general commerce that might have developed the country yet interfered with the almighty fur trade. Another thirteen years elapsed before steam power again roiled the waters of the Columbia River.

Before railroads came to dominate transportation across North America, the steamboat was the main mechanism by which steam power was introduced and spread through the United States, beginning with the voyage of the *Clermont* on the Hudson River in 1807. The *Beaver* reached the lower Columbia River twenty-nine years later, but not until the Army transport *Massachusetts* arrived under her own power in 1849 did the growing population of the Pacific Northwest fully grasp the wonders of steam propulsion. Only then did they learn how it might ease the burdens imposed by isolation from the rest of the United States by popularizing maritime connections and the Columbia River gateway.

Of even greater importance in the history of commercial transportation was the Pacific Mail Steamship Company's diminutive *Carolina,* which entered the Columbia River in mid 1850 on her maiden voyage up the West Coast. Carrying letters, cargo, and a few passengers, she paused at Astoria, six days out from San Francisco, then continued another two days to reach the tiny settlement of Portland. The *Carolina* brought the first mail to Oregon by way of the Isthmus of Panama. Until this time mail had been dispatched north to Oregon in sailing vessels and service had been irregular. The arrival of the screw-propeller *Carolina* marked the beginning of fairly regular service between Oregon and California.

When the *Carolina* first reached Astoria, a discerning observer might have noticed a home-built steamboat called the *Columbia* taking shape on

the riverbank. Her maiden voyage in July 1850 took her upriver to Portland and later to Oregon City, where the collective citizenry gathered to celebrate Independence Day and welcome the first true steamboat on Oregon waters. Except for the symbolism, the *Columbia* offered them little to brag about: ninety feet long, doubled-ended, and resembling a ferryboat, this strictly utilitarian vessel lacked both style and comfort. Her speed seldom exceeded four to five miles an hour. The *Columbia* made two runs a month to Astoria, connecting with Pacific Mail steamers from California. For passage, travelers paid twenty-five dollars each way and had to bring along their own blankets and lunch baskets.

Soon half a dozen steamboats joined the *Columbia* on Northwest waters. The first of any size was the *Lot Whitcomb* (160 feet long with two side-wheels, each eighteen feet in diameter). Built at Milwaukie, Oregon (and named for the town's founder and pioneer merchant and miller), she utilized technology developed in Europe and along the rivers of the East and Midwest. Launched on Christmas Day in 1850 amid great festivities, the *Lot Whitcomb* churned between Portland and Astoria twice a week and charged passengers a fare of twelve dollars, a substantial sum at the time.

A tugboat works a barge loaded with wood chips through the old locks at Bonneville Dam. Only two barges at a time could make the trip.

Portland's modern waterfront, where grain arriving by barge and rail is transferred to ocean-going ships bound for Asian markets.

It was during the formative decade of the 1850s that Portland emerged as the largest urban center north of San Francisco. The settlement also established effective control of an immense tributary area that encompassed both the Willamette Valley and the Columbia Plateau east of the Cascade Mountains. By dominating the main water routes, Portland maintained an advantage over all rivals even after the coming of railroads and the emergence of new population centers in Idaho's mining districts and on Puget Sound. Only Seattle, which got off to a much slower start in 1852, would eventually surpass Portland in population (first noted in the 1910 census) and regional importance—although the latter assertion remains a matter of heated debate and the basis for an ongoing urban rivalry.

Portland's busy wharves formed the heart of a rapidly expanding transportation network that linked lofty sailing vessels and ocean-going steamships from distant ports with the shallow-draft steamboats that shuttled cargoes and passengers along the Willamette and Columbia rivers. Freight destined for upriver points was transferred to river steamers or to the wagons that congested Portland's muddy streets. At the docks, during busy seasons, merchants, farmers, and ship captains congregated to trade information and goods and discuss business prospects.

The lower Columbia River is deep and broad, forming a water thoroughfare more than a hundred miles long between Portland and the sea, but steamboats attempting to ply the Columbia River above Portland faced formidable natural obstacles. Little more than thirty miles east of the confluence of the Columbia and Willamette rivers was the first of three stretches of white water that once forced Hudson's Bay voyageurs to undertake arduous and time-consuming portages. At first, little changed during the steamboat era; until 1896, travel still required two portages and three separate steamboats to travel up the Columbia and Snake rivers from Portland to Lewiston, gateway to the mines and forests of northern Idaho. Except for a rough, summer-only cattle trail built in the 1870s and known as The Dalles and Sandy Road, precipitous cliffs where the Columbia cuts through the Cascade Range made a land route prohibitively expensive to build.

A series of Indian wars in the 1850s encouraged the growth of steamboat traffic along the Columbia River. In the aftermath of a brief but vicious fight at the Cascades, a growing fleet of steamboats regularly plied the middle river, mainly to haul army supplies and soldiers, although each autumn they picked up emigrants who had reached The Dalles after the long journey west along the Oregon Trail. Prior to the late 1850s there was little traffic along the Columbia above The Dalles, but offering a hint of the dramatic changes soon to overtake the upriver trade was the flurry of mining excitement known as the Fraser River Rush of 1858. Many goldseekers came by ship from California to The Dalles, which served as an outfitting point for the upper Columbia River route to the British Columbia diggings.

When the Indian wars of the Columbia plateau ended in 1859, a well-organized steamboat service existed between Portland and The Dalles, even when attempts to probe the rivers of the upper country were just beginning. At the same time, a competitive free-for-all at the Cascades encouraged steamboatmen to forge a monopoly embracing the entire Columbia River between Astoria and The Dalles. To that end, they formed the Oregon Steam Navigation Company in late 1860. Into this grand consolidation went a pool of a dozen steamboats serving all portions of the

Columbia River below its junction with the Snake. As good fortune would have it, the Oregon Steam Navigation Company was ready when the big gold rush to Idaho began in the spring of 1861.

When news of a mineral bonanza in the northern Rocky Mountains reached Portland, it caused "a blaze of excitement" and encouraged a mass exodus of miners and merchants for the diggings. Prospectors idle in California and drifters who had been chasing elusive yellow nuggets since the days of 1849 swarmed north in search of gold. Argonauts came from all over the United States as well as from Mexico, Canada, Great Britain, Italy, France, China, and the Hawaiian Islands; and their ranks included churchmen, merchants, laborers, and lawyers, virtually anyone capable of handling a pick and shovel.

From 1861 to 1865 nearly every steamship heading north from San Francisco to Portland was crowded with gold seekers. Prior to the mining rush, messages, people, and goods all crossed the interior Pacific Northwest no faster than a horse or canoe, but the advent of steamboats on the upper Columbia and Snake rivers changed that, bringing in their wake the improvements that some observers equated with civilization. Not fifteen years

➤ *Another postcard image recalls the days of log rafts on the lower Columbia River. Courtesy Oregon Historical Society.*

earlier, the Clearwater Valley above Lewiston "was a howling wilderness, and a white man carried his life in his hands, who dared to venture in these parts," but traveling now by steamboat, noted one journalist of the time, "gentlemen seated on the forward guard view the scenery, smoke Havana cigars, and quaff Champagne cock-tails. The daily papers penetrate here, and St. Louis news is read here in seventeen days after date." It was a strange feeling, "that of whirling along by steam where so few years before the Indian and the trader had toiled through the virgin forest, bending under the weight of their canoes."

The primary beneficiary of the Idaho gold rush—the greatest excitement in the West since the California bonanza of the late 1840s—was the Oregon Steam Navigation Company. Prospectors, merchants, and gamblers crowded aboard its rapidly expanding fleet of steamboats; stowed on their lower decks were enormous cargoes of axes, shovels, tents, foodstuffs, whiskey, and other kinds of freight bound for the trailheads. Boats on their way downriver brought returning passengers and the yellow dust that was the source of all the excitement. As a result of the mining boom that dropped a windfall into its corporate lap, after only six months in operation

This postcard shows lumber awaiting loading at Longview, Washington. Courtesy Idaho State Historical Society.

the "financial wonder of its day" declared a twenty percent dividend, and that was only the promising beginning for what emerged as the far Northwest's premier business enterprise.

During its nineteen-year existence, the Oregon Steam Navigation Company amassed a fleet of more than thirty steamboats and paid out dividends of nearly five million dollars. Portland businessmen who organized the enterprise in 1860 succeeded beyond their wildest dreams and soon emerged as the city's moneyed elite. The company was literally a millionaire-making machine.

Although the mining excitement waned in the late 1860s, the Great River of the West was still the main transportation artery linking Portland with scattered supply centers and mining camps from The Dalles to Boise. It also served settlers living downriver as far as Astoria, Puget Sound via the Cowlitz River, and an overland portage north to Olympia. And still dominating the "Empire of the Columbia" was the Oregon Steam Navigation Company. During the 1870s, when golden grains replaced Rocky Mountain gold in the economy of the Pacific Northwest, the company's steamboats funneled a rising tide of wheat from the newly planted fields of eastern Washington and Oregon to Portland.

Every fall for nearly half a century after 1868, a fleet of tall-masted ships hauled sacks of wheat from the wharves of Portland to ports as distant as Cork, Queenstown, and Liverpool. Sailing ships continued to transport commodities from the Pacific Northwest, notably wheat and lumber, through the Columbia River gateway until well after World War One, although by the onset of the great depression in the early 1930s they had virtually disappeared. The last cargo to leave the Columbia River on a merchant sailing vessel was three million board feet of timber headed for Cape Town, South Africa, aboard the six-masted schooner *Tango* on May 2, 1942. Today the annual harvest of golden grain continues to travel down through the Columbia Valley, but it reaches Portland mainly by barge and by rail in covered hopper cars and is shipped from there by bulk carriers to markets primarily in Asia.

Certainly not all steamboat and steamship traffic on the lower

Columbia River was freight-oriented. Especially during the 1880s and 1890s, when an expanding network of railway lines challenged the riverboat monopoly, tourism played an increasingly important role in sustaining steam along the Columbia. The word "vacation" was not part of the vocabulary of a pioneer generation of Pacific Northwesterners, and paid vacations for the masses were still largely unknown when the new century dawned. But before then there were day-long and weekend excursions. Two routes in particular became popular excursion runs, attracting boats and services that catered primarily to pleasure seekers. From Portland up to the Cascades went tourists who wanted to spend a leisurely day sightseeing in the Columbia Gorge; downriver to Astoria steamed a more affluent group of people who wanted to spend a few days, or the entire season, at the seashore. Both routes attracted pleasure riders almost from the beginning of steamboating on the Columbia River, but the Astoria run was the first to evolve primarily into an excursion trip. Every summer a growing number of vacationers from the Willamette Valley traveled to Astoria and the ocean beaches of Oregon and Washington.

The Oregon Steam Navigation Company, ever alert to new business opportunities, ran special boats for vacationers as early as July 1862, when the *Jennie Clark* started once-a-week service between Portland and the coast. The few vacationers of the 1860s became the hundreds of the 1870s, and no longer would they all need to pack their own tents for the beach. The transportation magnate Ben Holladay built the Seaside House in 1873, where in addition to serving tourists, he entertained lavishly to impress prospective investors and Oregon's most influential citizens. The surrounding community of Seaside aspired to become the Pacific Northwest equivalent of the resorts of the East Coast, and by the 1880s it seemed that thousands of Portlanders now had time and money enough to spend a week at the beach, and nearly all of them chose Seaside.

Seaside kept growing, as did the beaches on the Washington coast reaching from Ilwaco. In 1889 a narrow gauge railroad started running trains there across the neck of the peninsula above Cape Disappointment; within a year service had been extended all the way to Nahcotta. At Ilwaco

BAILEY GATZERT

THE MOST LEGENDARY steamboat of all was the sternwheeler *Bailey Gatzert;* her career spanned the years 1890 to 1926. Leaving behind a trail of foam and a plume of black smoke from her tall stacks, she was fast, graceful, and elegant. The *Bailey Gatzert* was widely regarded as the crowning achievement of Pacific Northwest steamboat builders. During the summer of Portland's Lewis and Clark Exposition, the *Bailey Gatzert* ran excursion trips to Cascade Locks twice daily, at 8:30 A.M. and 5:30 P.M. The cost of a round trip was $1.50, which included meals (and sometimes an exciting, impromptu race with a rival steamboat). Such trips remained popular with Portlanders until completion of the Columbia River highway in 1916, which captured much of the tourist trade through the scenic gorge. The *Bailey Gatzert* left the Columbia River for Puget Sound in 1918 and served as an automobile ferry between Seattle and Bremerton until 1926.

Sheet music for the "Bailey Gatzert March" *(published in 1902 and dedicated to the management of the Lewis & Clark Centennial Exposition) hints at the widespread popularity of this Columbia River excursion steamer. Courtesy Columbia River Maritime Museum (1973.95.18).*

RIGHT: *The modern Bridge of the Gods at Cascade Locks. A natural bridge once supposedly spanned the river at this point but collapsed before the first non-native peoples reached the area.*

OPPOSITE: *An early twentieth-century steamboat excursion to Bonneville Park, a popular recreation site located near where the dam was later built. Courtesy Oregon Historical Society.*

the little trains met the steamer from Astoria or eventually Portland, operating according to a schedule set by the tides. Beginning in 1905—the year Portland held its Lewis and Clark Exposition—the ocean beaches of the Pacific Northwest witnessed the largest crowds of tourists yet. That year the Astoria boats could barely handle the throngs, and more and more steamers entered excursion service. The finest steamers, such as the *T. J. Potter, Hassalo,* and *Georgiana,* together with boats of more modest size and furnishings, conveyed thousands of tourists to Astoria while the new railroad from Portland brought thousands more.

The growth of steamboat tourism was only one of several major changes noticeable on the middle and lower Columbia River around the turn of the century. With the opening of the government locks at the Cascades in 1896, steamboat traffic between The Dalles and the Cascades was able to continue below to the tidewater section of the river, and after that date many of the finest steamers on the Columbia did an immense tourist business between Portland and The Dalles. For the first time, steamboats could travel through to either destination without having to unload at the portage.

Columbia River

The Cascade Locks themselves were impressive, and the sight of an occasional steamer passing through the canal and lock chambers was something no tourist wanted to miss. Nearby was a railway station where the Oregon Railway and Navigation Company (successor to the venerable Oregon Steam Navigation Company) had cleared out the brush in a grove of trees and fashioned "Bonneville on the Columbia River." In 1911 this popular picnic grove boasted a dance pavilion, refreshment stand, children's attractions, baseball diamond, trout fishing in the nearby Columbia River, and camping sites for groups and families. Some people arrived on special excursion trains from Portland, and others came by boat.

Despite the new emphasis on tourism, considerable freight, which included large amounts of fresh fruit from orchards that once stretched along the lower Snake River, continued to travel by steamboat. Completion of the Cascade Canal was only the first phase in a long-deferred goal of eliminating two troublesome portages between Portland and Lewiston. At long last, after ten years of construction, the Corps of Engineers completed The Dalles-Celilo Canal and opened it to navigation on April 28, 1915. Extending nearly nine miles and commanding a total ascent of 81 feet by means of five locks, it replaced a cumbersome portage railway. By means of the new facility—some would call it "the Panama Canal of the Northwest"—the Columbia River was now navigable year-round from the Pacific Ocean to Priest Rapids, a distance of about 415 miles, while the Snake River was navigable for light boats for eight months of the year nearly 200 miles from its mouth, or about 465 miles from the Pacific Ocean.

The early part of May 1915 witnessed a week-long celebration that began in Lewiston and ended in Astoria. Nearly all the senators, representatives, and governors of the Pacific Northwest states participated. Ironically, The Dalles-Celilo Canal had hardly been opened to traffic before steamboating on much of the Columbia River seemed to end. Excursion runs between Portland and The Dalles remained popular for a time, but above Celilo, steamboat service rapidly withered and died because of increased highway and rail competition.

Below The Dalles, steamers halted service one by one after the opening of all-weather highways removed tourists from excursion boats; at the same time, the completion of the Spokane, Portland and Seattle Railway along the north bank of the Columbia took freight and passenger traffic from the formerly isolated steamboat landings. Even efforts to coordinate river and highway freight service failed. In 1923, the last sternwheel packet gave up the run between Portland and The Dalles.

The Great Depression of the early 1930s also marked the end of eighty years of regularly scheduled steamship service between the lower Columbia River and San Francisco. Coastal liners like the *Rose City,* which went into service between Portland and the Golden Gate in 1908, provided elegant accommodations for travelers. For a brief time, from 1915 until the United States entered the First World War two years later, the Union Pacific's San Francisco and Portland Steamship company competed vigorously with the rival Great Northern Pacific Steamship company, which met trains for Portland at their northern terminus of Flavel (now part of Warrenton). Railroad baron James J. Hill was determined that his luxurious and speedy ships,

At the Port of Klickitat, just upriver from The Dalles Dam on the Washington side, logs headed to downriver mills are juxtaposed with Mount Hood.

the *Great Northern* and *Northern Pacific,* would equal or better the time of the Southern Pacific's best trains between Portland and California. And they did.

The end of scheduled steamboat service on the Columbia itself by no means eliminated all river traffic between Portland and Lewiston, nor did it diminish the demand for improved waterways. However, demands for hydropower and irrigation water attracted far more attention than the continuing cry for improvements to the river to better serve transportation needs. The first of the great Columbia River federal dams was Bonneville, completed as a New Deal project in 1938. In April 1947, work began on another massive dam, McNary, which when completed in 1953 blocked the river at Umatilla Rapids and created slack water all the way to Pasco to form a river highway for towboats and barges.

River transportation nonetheless remained in the shadow of railroads until the Corps of Engineers completed a total of eight dams and locks on the Columbia and Snake rivers during the 1960s and 1970s that rejuvenated the water highway between Portland and Lewiston. After the last locks opened in 1975, railroads actually found themselves at a rate disadvantage with barge lines for grain traffic from the interior Northwest as far east as Montana, where grain traveled by truck across the Bitterroot Mountains to Snake River ports.

Portland today remains the hub of the Columbia-Snake-Willamette river transportation system, a total of 534 miles of certified navigable waterways. In Oregon's largest city, barges meet the ocean-going ships that still transport grain from the inland Northwest to distant markets. About sixty percent of the grain reaches Portland by train; the rest arrives by barges and towboats, some of which have threaded the fourteen-foot deep channel extending inland to Lewiston. As of the late 1990s, about six hundred people were employed aboard the Snake and Columbia rivers' forty towboats and one hundred seventy-five barges. They moved nearly five million tons of grain, nearly four million tons of forest products, plus sizable quantities of petroleum products, fertilizer, and large intermodal containers, some of which contained frozen French-fried potatoes on their way from Idaho to restaurants in Japan. The Snake and Columbia rivers are normally usable by barge twelve months a year.

The early 1990s saw the revival of tourism between Lewiston and the sea, with several companies operating luxury vessels and week-long cruises. Most sightseers on the Columbia and Snake rivers today are impressed by the scenery, but they are also awed by the technological wonders along the way. Whereas Mississippi River locks typically provide ten to twenty-five feet of lift, the John Day lock lifts one hundred thirteen feet and is thought

On a bright November day on the Snake River above Lower Monumental Dam, modern tourists follow in the "Wake of Lewis and Clark."

Passengers go ashore by Zodiacs to explore the lower Palouse River, which is easily accessible by small boat from the Snake River. The cruise boat MV Sea Lion is at anchor in the background. Piloting the Zodiac is photographer Ralph Lee Hopkins.

74

Columbia River

to be the deepest lock of its type in the world. The locks at Ice Harbor and Lower Monumental dams on the Snake River each lift 103 feet. Few shipboard tourists pass through these chasms of concrete and steel without a camera in hand, though it is difficult to record the full size of the chambers with anything but video equipment. Many people are also awed by the powerhouses deep inside the dams, where the muffled rumble of turbines means that falling water is generating electricity that will illuminate homes as far away as Canada and California.

Congress created the Bonneville Power Administration in 1937 to market power generated by Bonneville, Grand Coulee, and other federal dams in the Pacific Northwest. Today Uncle Sam's thirty dams supply nearly half of all electricity consumed in the Pacific Northwest; and they do so at wholesale rates that keep the average household electric bill lower than those in any other region of the United States. The dams also benefit industries that are heavy electricity users. Back in 1941, the new Bonneville Power Administration hired folk singer and writer Woody Guthrie to compose music for a documentary film celebrating its accomplishments. During that

A heavy spring runoff in May 1971 makes Ice Harbor Dam appear to float above the mist of the lower Snake River.

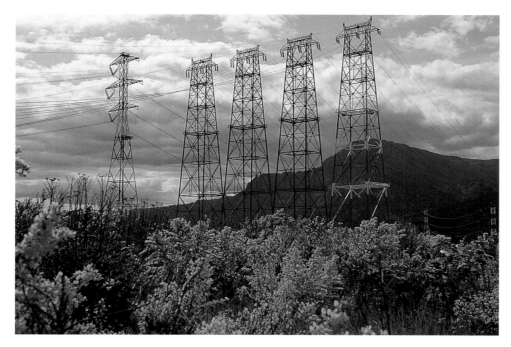

Cables spanning the Columbia Gorge near Bonneville Dam carry hydroelectric power to distant users.

WHAT'S SO GRAND ABOUT GRAND COULEE DAM?

GRAND COULEE DAM, unlike Bonneville, is not accessible to any cruise ships that ply the Columbia River; it is nonetheless a major tourist attraction, although its primary purpose is to generate electricity, provide water to irrigate farmland, and control floods. The building of Grand Coulee and Bonneville dams also created thousands of desperately needed construction jobs during the Great Depression of the 1930s.

"A surprising feature is the preponderant number of young men employed at Grand Coulee," observed the Oregon journalist (and later Senator) Richard Neuberger. "Waiting in line to eat in the mess hall, I noticed dozens of tall lads wearing football sweaters from near-by colleges and universities. The work is dangerous and scarcely a day passes without some one's being injured; fifty-four men have already been killed."

Grand Coulee, unlike Bonneville, was conceived as part of a vast irrigation project. Its twelve massive pumps would lift water from Lake Franklin D. Roosevelt to transform thousands of acres of parched, sagebrush-covered land in central Washington into a garden that boosters predicted would eventually support half a million people. The Columbia Basin Project first received water in 1951, and forty years later it remains an evolving network of pumping plants, reservoirs, and canals. As of the early 1990s the project contained some six thousand farms on nearly six hundred thousand irrigated acres that produce more than

A post-World War Two travel brochure advertises Grand Coulee Dam as a tourist attraction. Courtesy Special Collections, University of Idaho Library.

Visit GRAND COULEE DAM *and the* PACIFIC NORTHWEST

For complete information and travel plans, see . . .

WASHINGTON MOTOR COACH SYSTEM, 8th and Stewart St., Seattle
NORTHLAND GREYHOUND LINES, 509 6th Ave. North, Minneapolis

sixty different crops. The ultimate goal was to have slightly more than a million acres of irrigated land, but support for finishing the project waned during the 1970s and 1980s.

Columbia River dam projects, like most New Deal projects, are not without their critics. A Cayuse chief once told Neuberger that the "white man's dams mean no more Indians' salmon." He was partially right, but the situation could have been even worse, because the original design for Bonneville Dam did not include fish ladders and thus it would have blocked all salmon from spawning farther upriver. Only a public outcry kept upriver migration from being halted at that site. The fish debate in various forms continues to the present time.

Giant siphons at Grand Coulee Dam raise water to irrigate the half-million acres comprising the Columbia Basin Project in central Washington. Water returns to the river near Pasco. Courtesy Steve Eltinge.

When Grand Coulee Dam was finished in 1940, it stood as tall as a forty-six-story building and as wide as twelve city blocks. As the largest concrete structure on earth at that time it was often described as the Eighth Wonder of the World, and it became a popular tourist attraction. Others, however, would label Grand Coulee a white elephant and wonder how the thinly populated Pacific Northwest could ever use all the power it generated. The entry of the United States into the Second World War only months after completion of Grand Coulee Dam silenced the critics because a host of war-related industries, notably aluminum producers, needed all the power the dam could generate.

brief time of one month, Guthrie wrote twenty-six songs and earned $266.66. Best known of the series was "Roll On, Columbia," which the Washington legislature designated the state's official folk song in 1987.

Given the important link between water and electric power in the Pacific Northwest, it is worth recalling that the first examples of electric lighting in the region were all aboard steamships. When the *California* docked at Portland in the summer of 1877, its six arc lights, powered by the ship's engines, gave Pacific Northwesterners their first glimpse of the new form of illumination. Three years later, when the new steamer *Columbia* docked at Portland, the first of Edison's incandescent bulbs in the region cast a warm glow across the Willamette River. Who could predict back in the early 1880s just how dramatically electricity and its related technologies would change the landscape of the Columbia River as more and more dams were built to generate power?

OPPOSITE: *A night shot of round-the-clock work at Grand Coulee Dam in the late 1930s and early 1940s. Courtesy Minnesota Historical Society.*

BELOW: *The last light of an October day burnishes the sky above St. Johns Bridge, the last crossing of the main channel of the Willamette River before it joins the Columbia.*

CHAPTER FIVE

A River Landscape in Transition

Visitors new to the Columbia River often find it hard to sleep during their first night aboard one of the several cruise boats that regularly ply the waterway between Portland, Lewiston, and Astoria. Perhaps they need time to get used to unfamiliar sounds, like the sometimes noisy bollards that float up or down as the water level rises or falls in a lock chamber, affording a vessel a safe place to tie up. More often, though, they are excited by this chance to see for themselves the Great River of the West and the scenic wonders they could scarcely imagine. For travelers with an engineering interest, the huge dams and locks are objects of great fascination; others are drawn to the Blalock Islands near Umatilla in hopes of seeing unfamiliar species of birds that regularly migrate along one of North America's major flyways.

Once people become entranced by the waterway's visible landscapes, they almost always want to know more about the invisible ones that consist of important historical events, places, people, and processes no longer discernible. The more conscientious voyageurs will study various maps to compare then and now, ask many questions, and upon encountering some prominent landmark like Beacon Rock, an eight hundred-foot tall volcanic remnant that looms high in the mist below Bonneville Dam, hurry to the

OPPOSITE: *A modern cruise boat, the* Queen of the West, *heads upriver through the Columbia Gorge.*

A historic image of Beacon Rock. Lithograph from L. Samuel's Columbia River Illustrated *(Portland, 1882); courtesy Columbia River Maritime Museum (1978.83).*

ship's library to read what Lewis and Clark wrote about it in 1805 or 1806. Even the several bridges that span the modern river relate to its historic landscape.

As much as we might wish it, we cannot travel back in time, yet through visiting landscapes of historical significance we can go back to experience a place and make emotional connections between ourselves and the past. One of the enduring appeals of leisure travel along the river, either by boat or automobile, is learning about and exploring the Columbia's historic landscape, which includes not only Lewis and Clark and Sacagawea but also Gray, Vancouver, and a host of other interesting characters.

Like Sam Hill, for instance, a prominent but eccentric businessman who erected his Maryhill mansion on a high and treeless promontory overlooking the Columbia River opposite what is now the town of Biggs, Oregon.

🜲 ABOVE: *Sam Hill's mansion at Maryhill is now a popular museum.*

🜲 INSET: *"Stonehenge" is another of Sam Hill's creations on the banks of the Columbia River near what is now the eastern entrance to the Columbia Gorge.*

ENGINEERING NEW LANDSCAPES

BRIDGES AND HIGHWAYS

THE FIRST BRIDGE over the Columbia River within the United States opened at Pasco, Washington, in 1888 after the Northern Pacific Railway extended its tracks west to Tacoma and Seattle. The half-mile long structure, which marked the first time a railroad line crossed the great river instead of running its tracks alongside it, seemed to symbolize how the new mode of transportation was determined to forge new patterns of trade and commerce independent of the waterway. Downriver at the Cascades, The Bridge of the Gods is a graceful structure that since 1924 has permitted motorists to cross the Columbia above what was once the foaming Cascades. Its name derives from an Indian legend that recalls a massive stone arch that supposedly spanned the river at this point. Warring tribes (represented as brothers) angered the Great Spirit, who separated them by destroying their natural bridge. Curiously, this is also where the

— *The modern Bridge of the Gods.*

Columbia once flowed through a boulder-choked stretch of white water called the Cascades. It was above here that Lewis and Clark noted a drowned forest apparently created by a landslide in the Bridge of the Gods area.

Close to the mouth of the river is the last bridge to span the Columbia before it meets the sea, the nearly five-mile long Astoria-Megler bridge. Until it opened in 1966, ferryboats of various types linked the coastal roads of Oregon and Washington.

Perhaps even more dramatic was the coming of the automobile to the Columbia Gorge. Here was where rocky palisades that dropped nearly a thousand feet to the water's edge presented one final obstacle to pioneers who first headed their covered wagons west along the Oregon Trail in the 1840s. With the long-sought promised land of the Willamette Valley lying just beyond the Cascade Range, would-be settlers who had already endured nearly two thousand miles of challenges were forced either to risk their lives by taking the dangerous river in makeshift rafts or detouring south of Mount Hood along a primitive toll road. Even experienced rivermen hired by early-day fur companies sometimes miscalculated and drowned in the Columbia's massive falls, chutes, and whirlpools. The challenge was no less great for railroad builders in the early 1880s who used ropes to lower Chinese laborers down towering rock walls to drill and blast a narrow ledge for tracks of the Oregon Railway and Navigation Company (now part of the Union Pacific line that runs along the south side of the river).

The new Columbia River Highway was a sign of things to come. The Oregon engineer Samuel C. Lancaster designed the route to be beautiful as well as functional. After Oregon officially dedicated the section extending east to Hood River in 1916, the highway's spectacular engineering and aesthetic appeal attracted the world's attention. The first major paved highway in the Pacific Northwest also made automobile travel possible from Portland through the Columbia Gorge to eastern Oregon. This engineering marvel was completed between Portland and The Dalles in 1922.

Construction of the present superhighway through the Gorge in the 1960s destroyed portions of the historic route. Significant sections nonetheless remain intact and usable by any motorist willing to slow down and seek out the "Historic Columbia River Highway" that parallels parts of Interstate 84 and provides entrance to a series of moss-and-fern grottos and waterfalls that delight hikers and landscape photographers. Along one twelve-mile stretch of the old roadway, eleven waterfalls are either visible or readily accessible to motorists. In some places the sound of rushing water competes with that of Union Pacific freights rumbling along nearby tracks. One of the best places to obtain a panoramic view of the Gorge is from Crown Point. Located 733 feet above the river near the western end of the "Historic Columbia River Highway," this place offers a commanding thirty-mile vista.

A sign for the Historic Columbia River Highway at Crown Point.

At this place where "the sunshine of the East meets the rain of the West," he purchased seven thousand acres of land in 1907, hoping to build a Quaker agricultural community that would mature into a large city. Little came of his dream except Hill's "ranch house," a large building in the style of a French chateau that was solidly constructed of poured concrete for fire protection. Nearby, he also erected a concrete replica of England's Stonehenge as a World War One memorial. In 1917 Hill began the process of converting his mansion into a museum: he filled it with Rodin sculptures, which became the centerpiece of a massive collection of nineteenth century French Art. He even persuaded Queen Marie of Romania, the granddaughter of both Queen Victoria of England and Czar Alexander II of Russia, to travel to remote Maryhill in 1926 to dedicate his still unfinished museum. Today it is open to the public as the Maryhill Museum of Art.

Anyone who takes time to study the Columbia firsthand realizes that every portion of the river landscape is in transition. Abandoned sawmills and forsaken fish canneries have become increasingly common features

OF MOUNTAINS AND THE RIVER

*A*LONG MANY STRETCHES of the Columbia River, snowcapped peaks are visible in the distance. These mountains, seemingly so immutable, are also part of the river's changing landscape. Along the lower waterway, Mount St. Helens often seems to float on the distant horizon. Once the loveliest of Cascade peaks, at 8:32 on the morning of May 18, 1980, it stunned the nation and the world when it blasted away its crown with a force five hundred times greater than the atomic bomb that was dropped on Hiroshima in 1945. Speeding at up to 120 miles per hour, a superheated 650° whirlwind of heat, ash, and debris denuded two hundred square miles of heavily forested land within a fifteen mile arc to the north. All told, the combination of blast, fire, earthquake, and avalanche killed fifty-seven people, an estimated fifteen hundred elk, five thousand black-tailed deer, two hundred black bears, and literally hundreds of thousands of birds and fish. Massive mudflows down the Toutle and Cowlitz valleys filled the Columbia River's main channel, raising the floor from a depth of forty feet to a mere fourteen feet. This brought shipping to an abrupt halt. Since then Mount St. Helens has been relatively quiet. The Cascade Range includes several other dormant volcanoes, some of which have erupted within the past two centuries.

Another well-known Cascade peak is Oregon's highest promontory, Mount Hood. Standing 11,237 feet high, it forms a prominent part of the Columbia River landscape east of The Dalles and also upriver from Vancouver. From there Lieutenant Broughton and the men of the Vancouver expedition became the first Euro-Americans to be awed by the snow-covered mountain. It was named for Lord Samuel Hood, a member of the Board of Admiralty who signed the original instructions for the Vancouver voyage. It was this same expedition that named Mount St. Helens after the British ambassador to the court of Madrid.

Winter snows that accumulate in central Idaho near Grandjean will melt and flow into the Columbia River, mingling with waters that have been collected from all over the Columbia Basin.

along the waterway during the latter half of the twentieth century; each one of these industrial ruins testifies to massive economic change and dislocation. Consider too the fate of the mighty and picturesque cataracts at Celilo, east of The Dalles, where voyageurs of the Hudson's Bay Company once labored to portage their heavy bundles of furs and trade goods. All the white water is gone now. The falls, and a way of life for Indian tribes that fished there for millennia, disappeared in 1957 beneath the forty feet of slack water created by The Dalles Dam.

From the 1930s through the 1970s, dams were widely viewed as good

The geometric spillway at McNary Dam, located near Umatilla, Oregon.

Part of the effort to save salmon runs on the Columbia River is this maze of pipes and chutes at McNary Dam.

and useful legacies bequeathed to future generations. Young men in the 1930s dropped out of college for a year or two to join in the important and thrilling work of building Bonneville and Grand Coulee dams. During the Great Depression, both of these dams seemed to symbolize the triumph of engineering technology over wild and unpredictable nature. But by the 1980s and 1990s many Pacific Northwesterners would condemn these and other dams on the Columbia because of rapidly declining fish runs and the inadequacy of their supposedly limitless supply of electricity. In April 1992, the conservation group American Rivers placed the Columbia-Snake River system at the top of its list of the twenty-five most endangered rivers in the United States, mainly because of the hydroelectric dams widely believed to have caused a massive decline in the river's population of wild sockeye salmon.

Just below McNary Dam is a maze of sluiceways and multicolored pipes, some of which loop high into the air and to the untutored eye look suspiciously like an amusement park for fish. This is one highly visible part of a federally-funded salmon recovery plan: the purpose of the complex is to collect and load fish aboard barges that will take them past the dangers posed by dams. At one time it was believed that hatcheries alone would solve the problem of declining salmon runs. But during the last fifty years, even with hatcheries pumping millions of fish into the Columbia River system, salmon runs have continued to decline dramatically.

Again, some people believed the problem of salmon recovery was solved once and for all by the 1980 Northwest Power Act, which mandated that a four-state Northwest Power Planning Council bring back the remaining salmon population. The historic level, estimated to be sixteen million, was impossible to attain because whole river drainages have been blocked by dams built since the mid 1930s, but the council set out to increase the fish population from two million to five million. The amazing contrivance just below McNary Dam is part of the expensive and complicated recovery effort that has yet to achieve its elusive goal. So far, more than a billion dollars has been spent on salmon recovery.

Equally amazing but far simpler in design are the sailboards commonly found in the Columbia Gorge well downriver from McNary Dam. These constitute one of the best devices ever invented to coin wind into dollars (if only the salmon recovery plan could boast of similar technological success). For years settlers in The Dalles and Hood River areas had cursed the winds that howled through the Gorge, whipping the river's surface into whitecaps that spelled trouble. Gales sometimes forced steamboaters to tie up in sheltered areas and wreaked havoc with their passenger schedules. Although gusts of wind can still flip a semi-truck on nearby Interstate 84, sailboarders love the waves on the river, and their dollars contribute to a robust new economy in the Hood River area.

Once renowned mainly for the pears and apples that grew in a scenic valley in the shadow of Mount Hood, Hood River suffered a major economic setback in 1984 when the Diamond Fruit Cannery closed with a loss of more than three hundred jobs. Then the local timber industry slumped, causing a loss of still more jobs. But with windsurfing came an unusual form of economic windfall.

The transformation of Hood River offers a vivid example of how important tourism and outdoor recreation have become to the Pacific Northwest, helping replace dollars lost when the once basic extractive industries—the sawmills, mines, and canneries—shut down. Another good example of a long-term transformation can be seen at Paterson, Washington, on the Columbia River west of McNary Dam, where Columbia Crest's 2,100 acres of vineyards have emerged from the sagebrush covered hills of southeastern Washington. Wine, in fact, is one of the Pacific Northwest's newest industries, and numerous wineries have opened in the region. During the last three decades of the twentieth century, the wineries of Washington grew from a mere handful to more than seventy, and vintners now brag that they produce more premium wine than any other state except California, which remains far ahead. Much the same transition occurred in Oregon.

OPPOSITE: *Windsurfers sail back and forth across the Columbia River near Hood River.*

WINDSURFING FOR FUN AND PROFIT

THE EMERGENCE OF the Columbia River Gorge as a world-class windsurfing site is a relatively recent development, dating only from 1979. Today the Hood River area is the Mecca for windsurfers in the continental United States. All during the spring and summer months, wind tends to blow eastward off the cool Pacific Ocean toward the rising hot air of the inland deserts, rushing through the bottleneck of the Columbia Gorge and creating ocean-like waves that are the delight of windsurfers.

On a typical summer weekend this natural phenomenon attracts thousands of visitors to Hood River, White Salmon, Bingen, and half a dozen other sites where they zip their boards across the waves at speeds sometimes exceeding thirty miles per hour. Windsurfing has become big business in Hood River, but the numerous "boardheads" and their colorful sails that seem to flit like butterflies across the surface of the Columbia are a worry to towboaters: they push long and ponderous barges along the waterway and cannot stop quickly for any unlucky sailboarder who falls into the river ahead of them.

Regardless of the many changes occurring along the Columbia, as long as there is a Pacific Northwest, the Great River of the West will form one of its important landscapes—perhaps the defining one. In the Pacific Northwest, as in few other parts of the United States, regional identity is almost wholly linked to natural setting. Thus the Pacific Northwest without its mountains, rugged coastline, evergreen forests, and vast interior of sagebrush, rimrock, and big sky—and especially its Columbia River to link all these natural features together—is as unthinkable as New England without its Revolutionary War heritage, the South without its lost Cause, the Midwest without its agricultural cornucopia, or California without its gold rush.

Regional symbol, scenic wonder, natural resource, recreation getaway, transportation corridor, and object of environmental concern. The river is every one of those and so much more. Study the Columbia River in all its facets—read about it, explore along its banks, or visit a treasury of historical information like the Columbia River Maritime Museum in Astoria—and you will soon discover a gateway that leads to greater understanding of what the Pacific Northwest is today, how the region evolved in times past, and some of the major challenges its people face in the years ahead. Indeed, Roll On, Columbia!

➤ OPPOSITE: *Railroad tracks bridge the Great River of the West at Vancouver, Washington, to link Portland and Seattle and other shipping points.*

➤ RIGHT: *The cover of this 1927 tourist brochure issued by the Union Pacific Railroad evokes the popular image of the Pacific Northwest as a natural paradise. The railroad, which followed the south bank of the Columbia River through the Gorge, provided tourists an extended introduction to the river's landscape. Author's collection.*

A River Landscape in Transition

EPILOGUE

Columbia River: Gateway to the West began with a brief survey of the maritime landscape visible just outside the Columbia River Maritime Museum. Let us conclude by revisiting the museum itself. This is a wonderful place of discovery for young and old alike, and I use the word "wonderful" in the sense that starting with the soaring dimensions of its Great Hall, this museum evokes a sense of wonder in its visitors. These include well-traveled tourists who think they've experienced and learned all they need to about the Columbia during one of the several boat cruises that call at the museum. Many people enter the building with a somewhat jaded attitude of "been there, done that" only to be completely captivated by what they find. I recall visiting the Columbia River Maritime Museum in the company of a nationally-renowned authority on American maritime history, a man who knew all the world's great museums, and seeing him come away enthusiastic about the treasures he had found inside and how well they were interpreted.

Some visitors will be drawn to the lightship *Columbia*. As soon as they step on board they feel the river roll gently beneath their feet. Imagine how its decks heaved from swells created where the river meets the ocean, or try to put yourself in the place of Coast Guard crews anchored on the

OPPOSITE: *Buildings in modern Astoria appear to step up the hillside from the river's edge.*

97

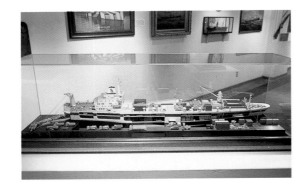

ABOVE: *This cutaway cargo carrier is one of many detailed ship models on display at the Columbia River Maritime Museum. This one depicts the States Line's RO-RO (roll-on, roll-off) freighter SS* Maine. *Columbia River Maritime Museum photo by Steve Eltinge (1982.21.1).*

RIGHT: *The Museum Store of the Columbia River Maritime Museum specializes in books, recordings, and numerous other items that relate to the sea and Northwest maritime history. Columbia River Maritime Museum photo by Steve Eltinge.*

Columbia River bar for weeks at a time to provide a guiding light and sometimes a refuge for boats in distress. Other visitors will marvel at the beauty of carved canoes used by Native Americans, their everyday fishing gear, reed mats, and many additional rarities. Or they may be especially drawn to the story of the industrial fisheries and canneries that grew up along the riverbanks and the many colorful cannery labels the museum has on display.

My favorite haunt, the part of the museum I usually go to first during my twice yearly visits, is where artifacts and stories of old steamboaters recall the time when the Columbia functioned as an early-day superhighway. As a result of inspiration gained this way, which so nicely complemented my river travels, I dug ever deeper into the colorful history of steamboating on Pacific Northwest waters until I had enough material for a book on the subject. That too is why I call the Columbia River Maritime Museum a wonderful place. Anyone who truly seeks to understand better the Great River of the West must start by experiencing the wonder it evokes—the wonder of its landscape and also its history. And the museum's artifacts and evocative displays whisper truths of the past to anyone who cares to listen.

The river is, of course, its primary artifact, and to tell the waterway's story across several centuries of human history is the reason why the Columbia River Maritime Museum continually adds to its large collection of maritime materials. That story, like the river itself, will not cease flowing through the life of anyone captivated by the Columbia's power and majesty. The Museum's Great Hall, several galleries, collection of books and photographs, and lightship *Columbia* collectively form an easily entered gateway to Columbia River history. I urge you to travel to Astoria and step inside the Columbia River Maritime Museum to feel for yourself the undeniable appeal of the Great River of the West.

The lightship Columbia (WLV-604) *served to mark the mouth of the Columbia River from 1952 to 1979. It is now open to visitors as part of the Columbia River Maritime Museum.*

= Red Wing =
"NIKG"
Portland   Oregon
Jan. 25, 1930

NOTES

8 Wilkes's descriptions of the Columbia River and Puget Sound come from Charles Wilkes, *Narrative of the United States Exploring Expedition During the Years 1838, 1839, 1840, 1841, and 1842,* 5 vols. (Philadelphia: Lea and Blanchard, 1845): iv, 293, 305, 378ff.

13 The description of the entrance to the Columbia River comes from Frederic Trautmann, ed. and trans., *Oregon East, Oregon West: Travels and Memoirs by Theodore Kirchhoff, 1863–1872* (Portland: Oregon Historical Society Press, 1987): 5.

22 The description of Astoria in 1874 comes from Charles Nordhoff, "The Columbia River and Puget Sound," *Harper's New Monthly Magazine,* 48 (February 1874): 338–48.

22 The abundance of salmon is described in John Mortimer Murphy, *Rambles in North-Western America from the Pacific Ocean to the Rocky Mountains* (London: Chapman and Hall, 1879): 25.

24 The description of mountain scenery along the Columbia River comes from the *Chicago Tribune* as quoted in the *Vancouver Register,* November 11, 1865.

OPPOSITE: *In January 1930 the Coast Guard Cutter* Red Wing *breaks ice on the Willamette River as it flows by Portland, Oregon's largest city. Courtesy Columbia River Maritime Museum (1964.170).*

A closeup and personal view of the prow of a large ship as it pushes upriver toward Astoria and the Portland-Vancouver area. Columbia River Maritime Museum photo by Steve Eltinge.

Notes

24   The description of Multnomah Falls is from Murphy, *Rambles in North-Western America from the Pacific Ocean to the Rocky Mountains,* 146.

37   William Clark's excitement at seeing what he perceived to be the Pacific Ocean is recorded in Gary Moulton, ed., *The Journals of the Lewis & Clark Expedition* (Lincoln: University of Nebraska Press, 1988): vi, 33.

43–44   Joseph Drayton's description of his 1841 journey up the Columbia comes from Charles Wilkes, *Narrative of the United States Exploring Expedition During the Years 1838, 1839, 1840, 1841,* and *1842,* 5 vols. (Philadelphia: Lea and Blanchard, 1845): iv, 293, 305, 378–91 passim.

49   The description of a fishwheel comes from Rudyard Kipling, *American Notes* (London: Standard Book Company, 1930 reprint of 1800 edition), p. 77.

53–54   The Pacific Northwest's first steamboat ride is described in Samuel Parker's, *Journal of an Exploring Tour Beyond the Rocky Mountains* (Minneapolis: Ross & Haines, 1967 reprint of 1838 edition): 310–11.

63   Descriptions of early steamboat travel come from the *Oregonian,* June 8, 1861 (first quotation); Fitz-Hugh Ludlow, "On the Columbia River," *Atlantic Monthly 14* (December 1864), 703–705 (second quotation).

66–70   The description of steamboat tourism is adapted from Randall V. Mills, *Stern-Wheelers up Columbia: A Century of Steamboating in the Oregon Country* (Lincoln: University of Nebraska Press, 1977 reprint of 1947 edition): 154–168.

76   An excellent contemporary account of building Grand Coulee Dam is Richard L. Neuberger, *Our Promised Land* (New York: Macmillan, 1938): 61–85.

66   Neuberger's comments on the decline of salmon come from *Our Promised Land,* 124.

SUGGESTIONS FOR FURTHER READING

THE FOLLOWING SHORT bibliography seeks to guide readers to my sources and suggests opportunities for further study of a specific subject. Some sources are mentioned only in the Notes.

Cody, Robin. *Voyage of a Summer Sun: Canoeing the Columbia River.* New York: Alfred A. Knopf, 1995. This modern adventure story transports readers from the source of the Columbia to its rendezvous with the Pacific Ocean.

Dietrich, William. Northwest Passage: *The Great Columbia River.* New York: Simon & Schuster, 1995. A detailed contemporary examination of the Columbia River.

Harden, Blaine. *A River Lost: The Life and Death of the Columbia.* New York: W. W. Norton & Company, 1996. An evocative personal look at the river's modern troubles.

Holbrook, Stewart. *The Columbia.* New York: Holt, Rinehart and Winston, 1956. A good popular account of the river and its history.

➤ OPPOSITE: *An abstract photograph of colorful net floats used by modern-day fishermen. Columbia River Maritime Museum photo by Steve Eltinge.*

Sparkling waters from one of several public fountains in downtown Portland symbolize the city's role as capital of the Empire of the Columbia.

Mills, Randall V. *Stern-Wheelers up Columbia: A Century of Steamboating in the Oregon Country.* Lincoln: University of Nebraska Press, 1977 reprint of 1947 edition. The best book to date on steamboats in the Pacific Northwest.

Morgan, Murray. *The Columbia: Powerhouse of the West.* Seattle: Superior Publishing Company, 1949. Recalls the optimism of the great era of dam building.

Mueller, Marge and Ted. *Fire, Faults & Floods: A Road and Trail Guide Exploring the Origins of the Columbia River Basin.* Moscow: University of Idaho Press, 1997. An illustrated geological introduction to the river.

Petersen, Keith C. *River of Life, Channel of Death: Fish and Dams on the Lower Snake.* Lewiston: Confluence Press, 1995. An examination of modern environmental problems encountered on the Columbia's main tributary.

Pitzer, Paul C. *Grand Coulee: Harnessing a Dream.* Pullman: Washington State University Press, 1994. A detailed account of building the Columbia's greatest dam.

Schwantes, Carlos A. *The Pacific Northwest: An Interpretive History.* 2nd ed. Lincoln: University of Nebraska Press, 1996. Places the Columbia River within the context of Pacific Northwest history.

Schwantes, Carlos A. *Long Day's Journey: The Steamboat and Stagecoach Era in the Northern West.* Seattle: University of Washington Press, 1999. An extended examination of the world defined by these two transportation technologies.

Timmen, Fritz. *Blow for the Landing: A Hundred Years of Steam Navigation on the Waters of the West.* Caldwell: Caxton Printers, 1973. Good visual history of steamboating in the Pacific Northwest.

White, Richard. *The Organic Machine: The Remaking of the Columbia River.* New York: Hill & Wang, 1995. A witty, erudite, and short introduction to the Columbia River today.

The lights of downtown Portland reflect across the Willamette River, which bisects the city.

ℐNDEX